BACKROADS

of

WISCONSIN

BACKROADS

—— of ——

WISCONSIN

*Your Guide to Wisconsin's Most Scenic
Backroad Adventures*

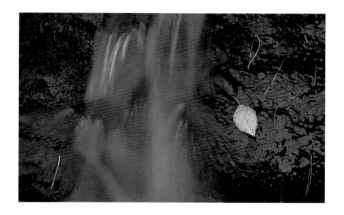

TEXT BY MARTIN HINTZ

PHOTOGRAPHY BY BOB RASHID

Voyageur Press

A Pictorial
Discovery Guide

DEDICATION

For the family . . . all travelers, all explorers—MH

For Robert and Daniel Rashid—BR

Edited by Margret Aldrich
Designed by Andrea Rud
Cover and maps designed by JoDee Turner
Printed in Hong Kong

02 03 04 05 06 5 4 3 2 1

Library of Congress Cataloging-in-Publication Data
Hintz, Martin.
    Backroads of Wisconsin : your guide to Wisconsin's most scenic backroad adventures / text by Martin Hintz ; photography by Bob Rashid.
        p. cm. — (A pictorial discovery guide)
Includes bibliographical references and index.
    ISBN 0-89658-513-1 (alk. paper)
    1. Wisconsin—Tours. 2. Scenic byways—Wisconsin—Guidebooks. 3. Wisconsin—Pictorial works. 4. Automobile travel—Wisconsin—Guidebooks. I. Title. II. Series.
    F579.3.H545 2002
    917.7504'44—dc21
                    2002002236

Distributed in Canada by Raincoast Books, 9050 Shaughnessy Street, Vancouver, B.C. V6P 6E5

Published by Voyageur Press, Inc.
123 North Second Street, P.O. Box 338, Stillwater, MN 55082 U.S.A.
651-430-2210, fax 651-430-2211
books@voyageurpress.com
www.voyageurpress.com

Educators, fundraisers, premium and gift buyers, publicists, and marketing managers: Looking for creative products and new sales ideas? Voyageur Press books are available at special discounts when purchased in quantities, and special editions can be created to your specifications. For details contact the marketing department at 800-888-9653.

ON THE COVER:
VILAS COUNTY ROAD K WINDS THROUGH SCENIC WISCONSIN.

ON THE TITLE PAGE, MAIN PHOTO:
THE ST. CROIX NATIONAL SCENIC RIVERWAY IS SEEN FROM SUMMIT PEAK AT INTERSTATE PARK.

ON THE TITLE PAGE, INSET:
A LEAF RESTS BESIDE FLOWING WATER AT AMNICON FALLS STATE PARK.

CONTENTS

INTRODUCTION

Wondrous Wisconsin is defined by its geography. The state is an alluring world shaped by glaciers and molded by eons of rascally weather that filed, pruned, clipped, washed, cleansed, and soaked the landscape. Wisconsin boasts five distinct topographies to delight both geologists on a scientific mission and visitors on a ramble: the Northern Highlands, Lake Superior Lowlands, Western Uplands, Central Plain, and Eastern Ridges and Lowlands. Of these five, all but the Lake Superior Lowlands encompass between 13,000 and 15,000 square miles apiece.

FALL COLOR SURROUNDS THE BRUNSWEILER RIVER.

The lake-dotted Northern Highlands contain the most extensive forests in Wisconsin, providing camping, woods walking, fishing, hunting, and related getaway possibilities. The Lake Superior Lowlands comprise a skinny strip of raw land in the far northwest part of the state, encompassing only about 1,250 square miles. These rough-cut ridges slope from the Northern Highlands to the pebble-strewn shores of Lake Superior and include marvelous waterfalls and berry-eating bears.

The Western Uplands are scoured by the Mississippi and Wisconsin Rivers, which cut through rugged cliffsides and provide vistas up to 1,700 feet above sea level. The region also has some of the state's most prized soil for farming. Rich and fertile like a dark flour, the loam makes a heavy blanket perfect for growing corn, soybeans, and fruit. The low-lying Central Plain in the heart of the state is a land of cranberry bogs, potato farms, forests, and the occasional wolf pack. The

Eastern Ridges and their related Lowlands provide a smoothly glaciated plain on which sprawls the state's largest urban concentration, stretching between Madison and Milwaukee.

Water is a key player in making Wisconsin such a varied and garden-like locale. With Lake Superior on the north, Lake Michigan on the east, and more than 8,500 mapped lakes, there is no dearth of water—or water-related sporting opportunities. A large portion of the state drains toward the Mississippi River, the mighty flowage that forms much of Wisconsin's western border. The Wisconsin River is the second-most impressive waterway, wending its boa-constrictor way to link with the rushing "Father of Waters." Other major waterways include the Eau Claire, Black, Chippewa, Fox, and Rock Rivers with their many tributaries leading to trout-rich backwaters or marshlands replete with bullheads and crappies.

Wisconsin's weather is all encompassing. If you don't like it one minute, hang on—it's bound to change shortly. In the autumn, it is a great media tradition for local television stations and newspapers to track the fall-color line as the leaves change in the far north and work their way to the south.

Since there is always snow in the winter, hardy residents have adapted well—if you can't lick Old Man Winter, you may as well join him. This means snowmobiling, ice fishing, cross-country and downhill skiing, sledding, and skating. After all, that's what fireplaces are for—to warm one's rosy cheeks after a day enjoying the frosty outdoors. The cold never fazes Milwaukee's Polar Bear Club, a mob of several thousand characters who think nothing of leaping into the frigid waters of Lake Michigan each New Year's Day. In the minds of the swimmers, the chillier it is, the better.

Yet spring is considered a favorite for many saner folks. Some love searching for secretively seasonal and delicious morel mushrooms. Others eagerly await the explosion of wild asters and irises on the prairies and wood violets, the state flower, at the forest fringe. Still more flock to Monches Farms and other off-the-beaten-path garden centers to stock up on vegetable sets and floral plantings.

Of course, lazy summer days are always special for anyone seeking solitude on the state's sleepy backroads. The color blue dominates the landscape at this time of year, as azure skies and aquamarine lakes and streams promise to chase away any philosophical or emotional "blues." Blue is also present in the mighty spruce, which is complemented by the herbaceous blue-green of its cousin trees.

The trees of Wisconsin's forests originally carpeted thirty million acres of the state's approximately thirty-six million acres. Loggers quickly took care of the old-growth pines and hardwoods in the northeast, while the northern conifers felt the teeth of the cross cut saws next. Millions of board feet of fresh lumber were rafted to mills downstream on the Wolf, Peshtigo, and neighboring rivers. Of course, that boom was finite, as the country's insatiable demand for more lumber quickly gave Wisconsin a buzz cut that took generations for recovery. Today, Wisconsinites are pleased that white pine, red oak, ash, cedar, maple, basswood, hemlock, jack pine, and other tree varieties have rebounded, but alert hikers and backcountry motorists can still find the remains of long-abandoned lumber camps and logging roads. These bittersweet reminders of the state's good old frontier days are now overgrown with chokecherry or raspberry bushes, but the songs and lore of that Paul Bunyan era live on.

In spite of the ever-expanding bloat of development, most of Wisconsin's animal life has generally adapted well to the squeeze. Even coyotes and fox have found homes in suburbia. There are challenges to the cohabitation of wilderness and civilization, of course. Deer-auto collisions are now one of the chief causes of traffic accidents throughout the state, so drivers need to continually be aware.

Wisconsin is carved with backroads that allow the traveler to investigate firsthand the state's natural beauty and colorful history. Be ready to explore, to discover, and to have fun. *Backroads of Wisconsin* provides a creative peek behind the trees, over the hills, across the lakes, and beyond the seemingly unlimited horizons of the Badger State. It also provides guidelines on what roads to take, as well as describes favorite attractions and places to stop for pondering the wonders of both ancient and contemporary Wisconsin.

Pack the car with your Wisconsin highway map and a copy of the richly detailed *DeLorme Wisconsin Atlas and Gazetteer,* which can be secured in most bookstores. Be sure there is film in the camera and that several extra rolls are tucked into the glove compartment. Bring healthy snacks for the kids, some fresh water for Fido, top off the gas tank, check the oil, and hit the road for a day or weekend driving excursion. Or, if the mood and time permits, extend your stay along the trail. A tip from the pros: avoid the freeways when possible and poke around the small towns, hike or pedal the trails, smell the wild roses.

Backroads of Wisconsin highlights the wonders discovered by the author and photographer on their journeys up and down the state and provides rich hints on what you may wish to explore—yet you should use this book as a launch pad for your own investigation of the Wisconsin landscape. The state's country roads and rural byways lead the curious into exciting adventures regardless of the season.

Driving these roads, it becomes obvious that the Badger State has much more to give than a generous serving of its famous dairy-fresh cheese—the state offers a grand getaway where nature's rich diversity is respected and well tended, and new adventures lie beyond each bend in the road. So who knows what you'll find while exploring Wisconsin's byways. Only one thing is certain—it's sure to be a marvelous trip.

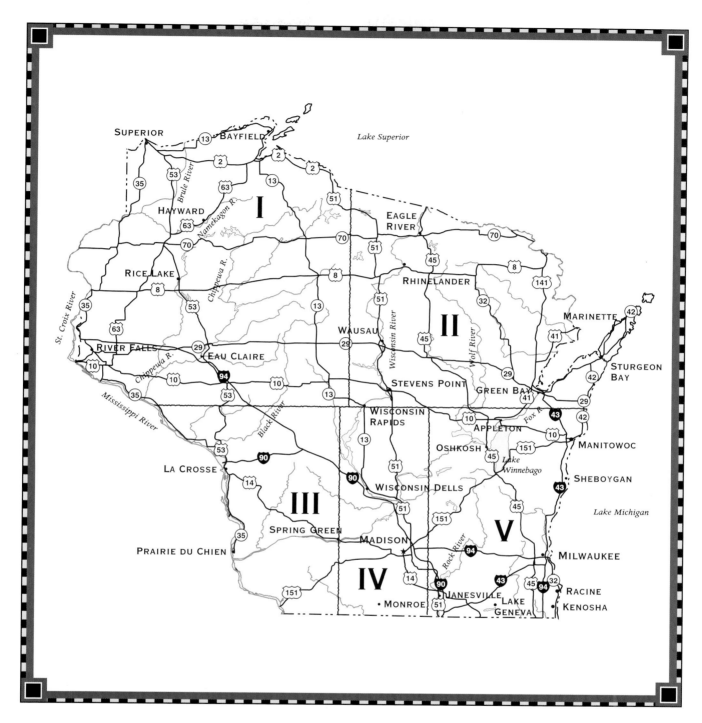

ABOVE:
NUMBERS I–V INDICATE THE REGIONS COVERED IN EACH
SECTION OF THE BOOK.

LEFT:
THESE PETROGLYPHS, THOUGHT TO BE THOUSANDS OF YEARS
OLD, WERE DISCOVERED AT ROCHE-A-CRI STATE PARK. THE
THREE LINES MEETING AT A POINT ARE PERHAPS AN ANCIENT
REPRESENTATION OF A BIRD'S FOOT PRINT.

PART I

THE NORTHWEST:
A QUIET ADVENTURE

FACING PAGE:
THE FOG SIGNAL BUILDING STANDS ON OUTER ISLAND, THE FURTHEST ISLAND FROM THE MAINLAND IN THE APOSTLE ISLANDS CHAIN.

ABOVE:
THE AMNICON RIVER SWEEPS BY A COLORFUL ROCK FORMATION IN AMNICON FALLS STATE PARK.

To find exceptional quiet in Wisconsin, the traveler should visit the far north and northwest reaches of the state.

At the Lake Superior shoreline, stand and peer into the rough-and-tumble surf where the lake meets the slower waters of the Amnicon, Poplar, and Brule Rivers. Off to the west is the city of Superior and its Minnesota neighbor, Duluth, with their extended docks that wait for plus-sized grain and ore carriers. But this shore, where polished, muted gray and reddish stones are tossed about in the cold water, is a place for reflection. Even the shouting of Big Manitou Falls, inland just a few miles, is not intrusive. Off to the east is Madeline Island, which Native Americans called home centuries ago and where tourists now flock. Despite the onslaught of visitors, Chippewa spirits still walk the island's birch groves on full-moon nights.

The stillness of the Chequamegon National Forest is palpable, too, especially when the pines sough in the evening. The trees talk over the day's events and if one listens close enough, you can often understand their conversation.

The same natural calmness extends downstate along the Wisconsin-Minnesota borderlands. Although the tumbling falls at Interstate Park bubble and roar in a mighty display, there remains a sense of solitude. Peering down from the lip of the chasm, with the St. Croix River far below, a human bystander is introduced to the real meaning of insignificance. It is enough to make anyone quiet.

THE LAKE SUPERIOR SHORELINE

THE ROUTE

Beginning in Bayfield, follow Wisconsin Highway 13 to Port Wing.

Wisconsin Highway 13 is the rim of the world—at least the Wisconsin world. The roadway runs northward from the Wisconsin Dells through the middle of the state to bounce around lakes, farms, and forestlands on its journey to the shores of Lake Superior. Once there, it juts off the Red Cliff Indian Reservation and ricochets west toward Superior. Then—at the northwestern edge of the state where it snuggles against Minnesota— 13 melds with U.S. Highway 53. The Highway 13 leg from Bayfield and the Apostle Islands and west to Port Wing is a blend of flat lakeshore frontage, the edge of the Chequamegon National Forest, and a few scattered villages.

From downtown Bayfield, the highway runs up a steep hill and then levels out on the way to the Red Cliff Indian Reservation. The tribal headquarters building of this band of Lake Superior Chippewa is one of the few large structures encountered in this region. Tribal worker Dennis Soulier points out that the reservation is "a good place to raise kids. We're close to the land, with lots of family around."

The reservation was the result of a series of treaties between the Chippewa and the United States, culminating in an 1854 agreement that was signed on nearby Madeline Island. There are approximately 4,000 registered members of the tribe, 1,900 of whom live on the reservation. As

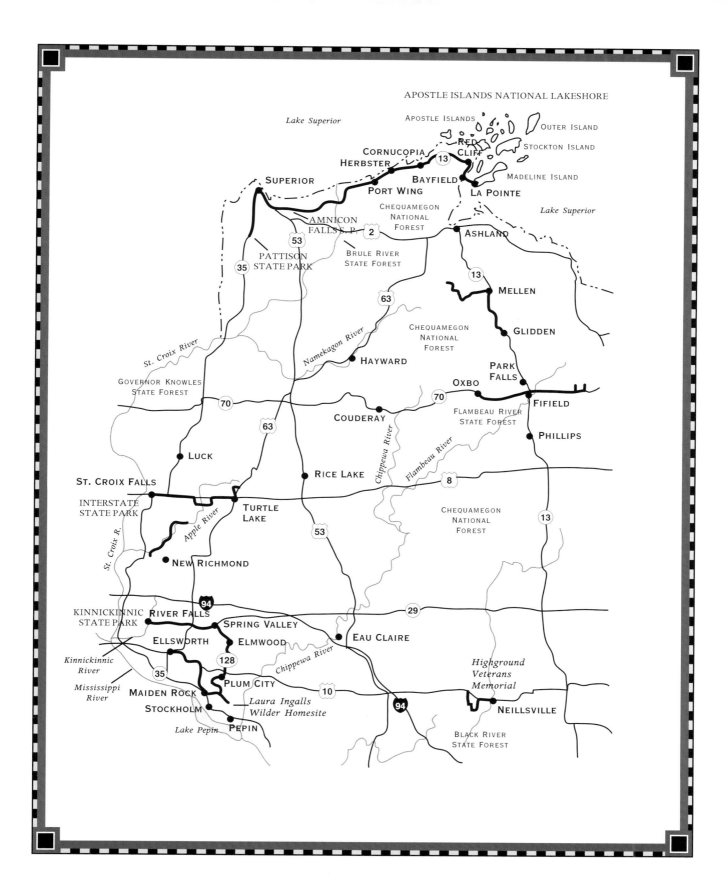

APOSTLE ISLANDS NATIONAL LAKESHORE

APOSTLE ISLANDS

Lake Superior

OUTER ISLAND

RED CLIFF

STOCKTON ISLAND

CORNUCOPIA

HERBSTER

13

SUPERIOR

BAYFIELD

PORT WING

MADELINE ISLAND

LA POINTE

Lake Superior

CHEQUAMEGON NATIONAL FOREST

ASHLAND

AMNICON FALLS S. P.

2

53

PATTISON STATE PARK

BRULE RIVER STATE FOREST

13

MELLEN

35

63

GLIDDEN

St. Croix River

Namekagon River

CHEQUAMEGON NATIONAL FOREST

PARK FALLS

HAYWARD

OXBO

GOVERNOR KNOWLES STATE FOREST

70

70

FIFIELD

63

COUDERAY

FLAMBEAU RIVER STATE FOREST

Chippewa River

Flambeau River

PHILLIPS

LUCK

RICE LAKE

8

ST. CROIX FALLS

INTERSTATE STATE PARK

TURTLE LAKE

CHEQUAMEGON NATIONAL FOREST

13

St. Croix R.

Apple River

53

NEW RICHMOND

94

KINNICKINNIC STATE PARK

RIVER FALLS

29

SPRING VALLEY

ELLSWORTH

ELMWOOD

EAU CLAIRE

Kinnickinnic River

128

Highground Veterans Memorial

Mississippi River

35

PLUM CITY

Chippewa River

MAIDEN ROCK

STOCKHOLM

Laura Ingalls Wilder Homesite

10

94

NEILLSVILLE

Lake Pepin

PEPIN

BLACK RIVER STATE FOREST

Devil's Island contains beautiful sea caves, made from centuries of wave erosion on the island's sandstone.

a boon to its economy, the tribe operates a public campground, from which several islands in the Apostles chain can be seen across the channel. The Isle Vista Casino—about a half-mile up the road on Highway 13—winks its tempting neon at passersby but taking area sideroads opens up more driving adventure.

Continue west, digressing briefly on Bayfield County Road K (Big Sand Bay Road) from Highway 13. Follow this gravel trail through the town of Russell as it heads north about two miles and then north on Raspberry Road to a turn west on Ridge Road. Proceed a short distance to the intersection of Blueberry Road and Ridge Road; turn north on Blueberry and west on Point Detour Road. Follow it to the rugged tip of land where you can see Raspberry Island to the northeast and Sand Island directly ahead. Several sand caves can be found in the vicinity and are best viewed by kayak or canoe. Retrace your drive to Ridge Road, turn west again and mosey over to Park Road leading to Sand Bay, which is on the shore of Little Sand Bay. There you can see how wave action has affected the shoreline over the centuries. Park Road will take you back to County K, which you can follow to again hook up with Highway 13 and continue your Lake Superior excursion.

A number of small towns wait to be explored as you continue on Highway 13. The first is Cornucopia. Several fishing sheds along the town wharf have been converted into gift and craft shops, where travelers can stock up on anything from fine-art paintings to antique porcelain stoves. Cornucopia was founded as a fishing village in 1902, when transportation along the shoreline was primarily by boat. On good days, however, a stage-coach from Bayfield would attempt the five- to seven-hour trek over a bumpy dirt path that became a quagmire every time it rained. Today, the little town has the northernmost post office in Wisconsin (ZIP code: 54827).

Near the Fish Lipps Restaurant, Helen Kaseno places cans of peas on a shelf inside Cornucopia's tin-roofed food market on Superior Street, the town's one-block-long main thoroughfare. A sign above the door reads "Ehler's Store—Where You Can Get Anything You Want." Kaseno is a second-generation Wisconsinite. Her father, Peter, came to town in 1905 from the Ukraine, one of hundreds of émigrés from czarist rule who settled along the lake at the turn of the nineteenth century. Settling after the forests had been clear-cut, the émigrés found work as farmers and fishermen.

Farther west, at the mouth of the Cranberry River, is Herbster, with several camping grounds close at hand for the road weary. The town is proud to say that it offers a "small town wilderness with a Superior view," referring to the lake that laps its northern limits. Neighbors in Herbster gather for a massive smelt fry the third weekend in April and a corn feed the first weekend in August.

Port Wing is the next major town on the roadway. It was founded in the late 1800s by commercial fishermen who were attracted by the natural harbor. The Flag River on the east side of town flows directly into Lake Superior, while Larson Creek goes through Port Wing and reaches the great lake via Bibon Lake. In the town's central park, take a close look at the small garden structure, which was made from the belfry of the old South Shore School—one of the first consolidated school districts in the state. The school was constructed in January 1903 to attract youngsters from around the area and hold down education costs. The district's "school bus" was a caramel-colored, canvas-topped horse-drawn wagon. In the rugged winters, sleighs were used to haul the students.

Port Wing is still an active commercial fishing hub, with several boats docked in its harbor. The doughty Julie Ann, which was first launched in 1944, bobs in a slight mid-afternoon swell, having just returned with a load of chubs and herring. Her crew had left a half-hour before dawn and chugged out about four miles on the raw November waves of Lake Superior to set nets. Back safely, it is now time to clean fish—hundreds of pounds of fish—all by hand.

Inside the tight confines of the vessel, sharp knives flash and scales fly as the catch is sorted, gutted, and packed in boxes to be sent to seafood-delivery outlets downstate. In a corner near the wheelhouse, an ancient wood-burning iron stove casts a fitful warmth. With snow expected, Captain Chris Johnson is glad to be back in port as he rubs his chapped hands to warm them.

Looking through a porthole, Johnson sees the wind slapping the waters of the bay into white-capped foam. The deck beneath the crew rocks even though the Julie Ann is tightly moored, and the men bend down to their tasks.

They know it will be rough on Lake Superior tomorrow.

Big Manitou Falls

I hear the oration of Gitchee Manitou, the Great Spirit. Don't tell me that I don't, or that I'm superstitious. If you come, you, too, can listen, and perhaps you will believe. His rumble is audible from a quarter-mile away the minute I stop the car and get out at the 1,376-acre Pattison State Park. I am thirteen miles south of Superior and the voice from Big Manitou Falls is calling.

I have driven across the northern rim of Wisconsin along Wisconsin Highway 13, picking up Wisconsin Highway 35 south to the park. The percussion of the roaring waterfall is enough to confirm that something much bigger than me is near.

I amble along a park sidewalk—apparently the only guest here on this blustery, November day—past a sign pointing the way to the ice machines and shelter house/nature center, then down a flight of steps to observe squadrons of tough-talking Canada geese that honk impudently as I pass.

THE ROUTE

Take Wisconsin Highway 13 west from Port Wing to Superior. At Superior, follow Wisconsin Highway 35 south to Pattison State Park.

ABOVE:
BIG MANITOU FALLS THUNDERS THROUGH PATTISON STATE PARK.

FACING PAGE:
THE WATER NEAR AMNICON FALLS APPEARS DIPPED IN GREEN FROM THE REFLECTION OF THE
SURROUNDING TREES AT AMNICON FALLS STATE PARK.

The walkway to reach Big Manitou Falls, Wisconsin's highest waterfall, passes through a tunnel under Highway 35, with the rush of traffic overhead echoing in the concrete chamber. But the autos' sounds can't match the waterfall's natural noise, which increases as I get closer. The thundering increases in volume as I proceed to the first of several overlooks into the 165-foot-deep gorge. A sheen of ice coats the next steps and—not being one to spend a lot of time hanging nervously over slick precipices—I step back, awed by the sheer volume of water plunging into the crevasse. The noise is deafening as the foaming Black River disappears over the rocky ledge, its roar saying goodbye in no uncertain terms.

The geography of this area was formed billions of years ago, due to volcanic action, erosion of the pervasive red granite, and glacial movement. Ten thousand years ago, melting glaciers formed a hundred-foot-deep lake here, but now there is just the mighty waterfall—the fourth highest in the United States east of the Rocky Mountains. Several vantage points provide excellent photo angles, without the danger of creeping close to the cliffside where the river slides away. The sight is, simply put, amazing.

Several hiking trails in Pattison get visitors out and about through the spread of forest, river, and boulders. The Big Falls Hiking Trail runs about a half mile past the main falls to dead-end at the park perimeter, where the much-calmed Black River flows away. The Beaver Slide Nature Trail is a two-mile jaunt that shows off the park's best flora and its resident fauna. You might be lucky to see rabbits, field mice, or other denizens of the surrounding forest. Overhead, keen-eyed hawks keep watching, just in case something small and furry makes a mistake and stays too long in the open. The longest hike in the park is the Logging Camp Trail, which cuts in and out of the trees and traces the riverbank, covering 4.7 miles. The trail's distance might be a chore for the littlest in your party, but it isn't a hard walk.

At the end of my adventures at Pattison State Park, the blustery weather necessitates that I turn up the collar of my coat and hunker down into its layers. On the long, meditative stroll back to the parking lot, I reflect on the voice of the waterfall—the Great Spirit—and wonder what it wants to tell me. Ultimately, I figure that the message I received is best kept as my secret, because everyone who tunes in to the voice of the falls will receive a personalized, special gift—one that best remains in the heart. And what more can anyone ask.

EVEN WISCONSIN'S SMALLER FALLS ARE FUN TO FIND.

WISCONSIN'S HIGHEST WATERFALLS

Of the state's sixty-two major identifiable waterfalls, these nine are among the most spectacular because of their height:
Big Manitou Falls, Douglas County, 165 feet
Morgan Falls, Ashland County, 90 feet
Superior Falls, Iron County, 90 feet
Potato Falls, Iron County, 90 feet
Copper Falls, Ashland County, 40 feet
Peterson Falls, Iron County, 35 feet
Brownstone Falls, Ashland County, 30 feet
Little Manitou Falls, Douglas County, 30 feet
Foster Falls, Iron County, 25 feet

MADELINE ISLAND

The sharp stars overhead are brilliant pinpoints, stabbing down on still-sleeping Bayfield. In the minus-25-degree weather, the frostiness that stills the air freezes mustaches and thickens blood. Thick-soled thermal boots crunch the snow as snowmobilers leave their warm motel for a midwinter 4:30 A.M. run along an ice bridge from Bayfield to Madeline Island—the largest island in the Apostle Islands region at fourteen miles long and three miles wide. The lake generally freezes here between December and April, allowing cars, trucks, and snowmobiles to lumber back and forth the mile or so between Bayfield and La Pointe, the largest year-round occupied village on the island.

Taking the ice road is a popular winter activity for hardy folks who come from around the Midwest to sample the snow and cold. The trip takes about thirty minutes, but be sure to allow time to tour the island before returning to Bayfield. Since few people live on Madeline during the off-season, the sound of snowmobiles isn't a nuisance.

The frozen road is regularly plowed between January and the first signs of thaw; it is formed by ridges of snow that serve as markers. After the year-end holidays, some helpful local folks stick their used Christmas trees into these snow piles as additional navigational aids. The year-round population of Madeline—the only island in the Apostles with any commercial development—hovers around 180, most of who live inland. More than 2,500 folks live here in the summer, however, and enjoy a community with an elementary school, police force, town council, restaurants, shops, historical and natural attractions such as Big Bay State Park, with its picturesque sandstone bluffs and 1.5 miles of shoreline.

The Apostle Islands are spits of land officially considered an archipelago—a succession of islands dappled across a broad stretch of water. In 1970, Congress named twenty of the islands and 2,500 acres of the Bayfield Peninsula a lakeshore to be managed by the National Park Service. While Madeline Island is part of the Apostles, it is not part of the lakeshore group managed by the National Park Service.

A summertime run to Madeline is best done on the ferry line, which makes several daily trips across the 2.6-mile-wide North Channel that separates the island from the mainland. The vessels are powered by muscular Cummins and Caterpillar engines, ranging up to 540 horsepower, and are capable of carrying a fleet of vehicles. The ferryboats are large, stable, and generally able to make their runs until the ice brings a halt to the season. Traveling by ferry is a social occasion, allowing island residents some casual time to chat among themselves as they make the routine trip. Tourists take photos, truck drivers relax, and kids shout to each other over the engine noise about their classwork.

In the shoulder seasons, an unheated, propeller-driven wind sled scoots across the ice, plowing over any open lake water. Everyone huddles together to get out of the wind, which whips around angrily trying to

THE ROUTE

In the winter, take the ice road that connects Bayfield to La Pointe on Lake Superior's Madeline Island. In the summer, take the ferry across the North Channel from Bayfield to Madeline Island.

Before the ice highway has frozen to a thickness safe enough for automobile traffic, the only method of travel for passengers and supplies is this wind sled. Here, driver Ron Nelson talks with a passenger before the last run of the day.

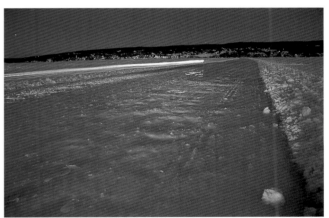

ABOVE, TOP:
A SIGN AT THE BEGINNING OF THE ICE HIGHWAY STANDS AS A WARNING TO MOTORISTS.

ABOVE, BOTTOM:
THE ICE HIGHWAY RUNS FROM BAYFIELD TO MADELINE ISLAND.

find any exposed skin between pulled-down stocking caps and upturned coat collars.

Wise boaters here carefully check the weather conditions before setting out to one of the Apostles. Even the ferry captains take such precautions. I was once stranded on Michigan Island for a couple of days when a storm blew up and blocked passage back to the mainland. I had to hole up in the lighthouse keeper's old home with two volunteer Park Service employees. Our only link to the outside world was their two-way radio, with messages crackling back and forth about the height of the waves, the wind velocity, and related weather data. Touring the beach after the storm, I found huge tree trunks and other refuse tossed up on the sand, attesting to the storm's ferocity. A Park Service boat arrived when the water had calmed enough, bringing much-appreciated supplies to the guides who stayed there all summer. Wading hip deep into the surf, I was plucked aboard and sped back to Bayfield.

The closed world of the Apostles provides an excellent research arena for scientists. Hiking Stockton Island, outdoors lovers will find the largest concentration of black bears in the world, whose strong-swimming ancestors paddled out to the island years ago. Since 1984, almost 140 shaggy *Ursus (Euarctos) americanus* have been tagged on Stockton, some of which were fitted with radio transmitting collars to continually mark their whereabouts. That figure makes a density of 2.1 bears per square mile on this island, compared with the average of one bear per square mile on the nearby mainland. Anybody seeing a bear is requested to make a report to the resident ranger, who logs the sightings on a large map in the island's visitor center. This helps the staff keep track of where the bears are, both as a warning to visitors and to plot the animal's movement. The island covers 10,054 acres, making it one of the largest in the Apostles. Botanists and biologists appreciate the diversity here, reveling in the contained ecosystem.

The Apostles are a delight with their wildlife vistas, recreational opportunities, and folks willing to share their experiences of island life. Be aware, however, that any guests visit here on nature's own terms.

CHEQUAMEGON NATIONAL FOREST

Driving through the pine-thick Chequamegon National Forest is a lesson in 4x4 downshifting. Puckerbrush reaches out on all sides of the trails through the woods, and the deep gullies and steep hillsides are difficult to maneuver. Of course, bears have no trouble negotiating these backcountry pathways high on the ridges of the forest's Glidden District, but it is different for autos or trucks. Most roads in the forest are hard surfaced, however, and primary paved highways like Wisconsin 77 run east and west through the forestland making for a generally smooth journey.

THE ROUTE

Start your drive in Glidden and proceed north on Wisconsin Highway 13 to Mellen. From there, take County Road GG west to any one of a number of marked forest road entry points to find the North Country Trail. Continue west on GG to the Mineral Lake Campground and turn north on Forest Road 187. Follow 187 as it winds past the Lake Three Campground to pick up Forest Road 199. Drive west on 199 to reach parking and hiking trail access to Morgan Falls and St. Peter's Dome.

Glidden, the self-proclaimed Black Bear Capital of the World, is a town that still offers a reward for anyone bringing in a bagged bruin bigger than the 665-pounder shot in 1963 and on taxidermic display in a case next to a local gas station.

The Chequamegon forest covers about 1,050,000 acres, with a net of almost 840,000 acres of publicly owned land. "Chequamegon" (pronounced Show-wa-me-gon) is Chippewa in origin. "Che" means water, "qua" is shallow, and "gon" is place— literally translating to the "Place of the Shallow Water." Chequamegon Bay, on the forest's north shore, is only several hundred feet deep, shallow compared to the 1,000-foot-plus depths of Lake Superior. In addition to Ashland County's Glidden district, other ranger jurisdictions include Park Falls in Price County, Medford in Taylor County, Hayward in Sawyer County, and Washburn in Bayfield County. Within these scattered sites, are the Moose, Torch, and Chippewa Rivers.

ICICLES AND MOSS BRIGHTEN A ROCKY LEDGE IN THE CHEQUAMEGON NATIONAL FOREST.

The demand for lumber in the Midwest spelled doom for Wisconsin's great northern forests. Logging continued well into the 1920s, when a dwindling supply of quality trees and the economic crunch of the Great Depression finally brought the industry to its knees. The timber companies sold off thousands of acres to folks seeking a better life, hoping that farming could replace the logging industry. Yet the soil was not suited for crops, and many frontier farms failed. Almost 1.5 million acres were abandoned by the 1930s and were available for sale at only a few dollars an acre.

The government stepped in and purchased much of the "wasteland," adding the area to its growing list of national forests. On November 13, 1933, President Franklin D. Roosevelt officially named the Chequamegon, and administratively cut it from the western part of the old Nicolet National Forest. Teams of young Civilian Conservation Corps (CCC) workers then were sent in to improve roads, bridges, dams, and recreational facilities in the new forest.

Driving the Chequamegon is viable even for beginners and moderately advanced 4x4ers who want a bit of a challenge on the rolling hills off the highway. Motoring in the forest is more of a means to an end—as a way to get to a camping site, an overlook, or a hiking opportunity—so stay on marked roads and avoid the posted hunter trails.

A DUSTING OF SPRING SNOW MELTS IN A POOL AT MORGAN FALLS.

ABOVE:
FALLEN LEAVES REST ALONG THE PATH TO MORGAN FALLS.

To observe the woods and water, hike the North Country Trail—a sixty-mile scenic route that slices through the Glidden, Hayward, and Washburn districts of the forest. That jaunt begins on Forest Road 390, two miles west of Mellen, and ends at County Road A near Lake Ruth, some five miles south of Iron River. The northern part of the trail is hilly, with the eastern half being the toughest. This section cuts through the scenic Penokee Hills, whose rock outcroppings and overlooks make the trip worthwhile, no matter how hard it is to reach them.

One of the geological attractions within the forest is St. Peter's Dome, a red granite hump near the northern edge of the forest's Glidden District, thirteen miles west of Mellen. The dome can be reached via GG, Forest Road 187, and Forest Road 199, which is the main road fronting the nine-mile square section of land that encompasses the dome and neighboring hills. Parking is available at an old quarry near the mound, with hiking trails leading to the 1,600-foot summit. From the top, a keen-eyed observer can spot Lake Superior's Chequamegon Bay twenty miles to the north.

HARDWORKING LUMBERMEN POSE ON A LOGJAM ON THE CHIPPEWA RIVER IN THIS PHOTOGRAPH FROM 1906. (MINNESOTA HISTORICAL SOCIETY)

Morgan Falls is along the walk to the crest, with the rush of water falling seventy feet into a pool. The waterfall is only about a half-mile from the parking lot and a mile from the top of the dome.

There are many other excursions in the Chequamegon area that you can explore beyond the trip outlined here. If you want to take a self-guided auto tour of the Moquah Barrens in the Washburn Ranger District, drive north on Highway 13 from Mellen to Ashland, pick up U.S. Highway 2 and go west to Forest Road 236, where you can begin your drive. "Barrens" simply refers to the glacial outwash, a sand and gravel soil covered with pines, blueberry bushes, and bracken fern. Many of the shrubs need roots up to ten feet deep in their search for water. The Forest Service is restoring the barrens to its more natural condition by removing many of the pine plantations and encouraging wild grass and prairie flowers to flourish amid small stands of trees. Interpretative stops along the route are marked with numbered Forest Service signs, beginning at the intersection of U.S. Highway 2 and Forest Road 236.

Another route will take you to the southern edge of the Chequamegon. One of the best-developed campsites in the forest is at the Mondeaux Flowage, which straddles the Ice Age Trail. To find the Mondeaux Flowage from Glidden, drive south on Highway 13 about seventy miles to Westboro. Turn west on County D and proceed to County E, where you will turn south to pick up Forest Road 1563. This will take you to the Mondeaux Flowage Dam Recreation Area. A giant esker (which forms the winding ridge of gravel and sand deposited by a stream that once flowed under one of the ancient glaciers) lies along the western rim of the lake. A hiking path goes along the crest of the esker, allowing a fine view of the surrounding forest. Other highlights along the trail include a mature white spruce stand about a mile or so to the southwest, followed quickly by a large bog, another esker, and a high ridge stand of old growth hemlock.

FLAMBEAU RIVER STATE FOREST

This adventure begins in Oxbo, Wisconsin, which sits on the intersection of Wisconsin Highway 70 and the Flambeau River in the midst of Sawyer County's Flambeau River State Forest.

The 90,000-acre forest spreads along the river's north and south forks, where canoeing is a favorite pastime. Experienced canoeists who know the river well encourage taking a river trip in sections, as distances can be deceiving. The link between Nine Mile Creek and Oxbo Landing, for example, is twelve miles, so travelers should count on at least a three-hour trip—one that is easy going downstream but a pain going back after a full day on the water. Plan on taking advantage of one or more of the fourteen campsites along the way that are reserved for the water-borne traveler. Proceeding farther along the river introduces some rough water, with the Flambeau Falls, Cedar Rapids, and the four-foot drop around Beaver Dam providing some stomach-churning thrills.

Cross-country skiing is a winter's delight in this area. For some of the best leg-stretching skiing, try the David D. Klug Flambeau Hills Memorial Ski Trail, a pleasant pathway swishing along for 14 miles from County Road W to 70. Also recommended is the 8.5-mile Oxbow Ski Trail that runs north of 70 along the Flambeau's North Fork. This leg starts simply and then fools you by getting plenty rough toward the end.

The Flambeau's mixed hardwoods and pine make perfect cover for a hiker, as well. There are many ways to access the woods. Among the best are along Price County Road W to the south of Oxbo, adjacent to the bog lands and spruce coverings of the Kimberly-Clark State Wildlife Area on Price Lake Road.

About 20 percent of the Flambeau River State Forest is in a state-mandated "no-cut" area, with a quarter-mile buffer on either side of the Flambeau River to protect the area's natural state. In some parts of the forest—best found by simply hiking along any of the trails around the Lake of the Pines and Connor Lake campgrounds—piles of cut brush are strategically placed to provide homes for shy forest critters. Connor Lake facilities are accessible for the physically challenged, allowing everyone the opportunity to enjoy that much needed breath of outdoors.

After communing with nature at Flambeau, travel east on Highway 70 from Oxbo to the bustling intersection of Wisconsin Highways 13 and 70 in downtown Fifield. On broiling summer days, the crowded intersection has all the appearance of a rustic Times Square. Even in the heart of winter, the same corner is just as packed with vehicles hauling snowmobiles or overloaded with skis and poles. In the autumn hunting season, almost every driver wears blaze orange. In spring, fishing fans crowd to

THE ROUTE

From Oxbo, take Wisconsin Highway 70 east to Fifield. Continue east on 70 to Forest Road 148, where you will divert north to the Smith Rapids Covered Bridge. After returning to Highway 70, resume traveling east. Turn north on Forest Road 144 and drive until you reach the Round Lake Logging Dam in the Pike Lake district.

LEFT:
THIS VIEW COMES FROM THE ROUND LAKE LOGGING DAM ON FOREST ROAD 144, OFF WISCONSIN HIGHWAY 70.

ABOVE:
THE SMITH RAPIDS COVERED BRIDGE SITS ON FOREST ROAD 148, OFF WISCONSIN HIGHWAY 70.

HARD ART TO VIEW

Just fourteen miles south of Fifield is Phillips, home of the Wisconsin Concrete Park where Fred Smith created more than two hundred figures of hand-mixed cement studded with broken glass, shattered mirrors, and other objects. At the park, you can go eye to eye with a moose and admire angels. Just don't touch.

Smith, a Price County native born in 1886, was an engaging fellow who started assembling his folksy art pieces at age sixty-five. The project took fifteen years after his 1948 retirement; he had worked as a tavern owner, lumberjack, dance hall musician, farmer, carpenter, and a host of other occupations over his lifetime. Smith slowed down his endeavors only when he suffered a stroke in 1964. He died in 1976 at the age of ninety.

FRED SMITH'S CONCRETE PARK STANDS AS A TRIBUTE TO ONE MAN'S CREATIVITY.

the North Country. Ready and eager for fun, the crowds at the intersection disperse east to the Chequamegon National Forest, west to the Flambeau River State Forest, or north to the Apostle Islands. Some might have already explored the numerous chains of lakes to the south and are looking for bigger fish and rougher trails.

For another leg of a North Woods journey, continue east on Highway 70 from Fifield to Forest Road 148 and the Smith Rapids Covered Bridge. This is the only glue-laminated structure in Wisconsin. The bridge is adjacent to the Smith Rapids Campground in the heart of the Chequamegon National Forest. In the winter, the span is a popular spot for camera-toting snowmobilers.

After visiting the bridge, drive east to the Round Lake Logging Dam on Forest Road 144 in the Pike Lake district. The dam is one of the few remaining wooden dams in Wisconsin, originally built in 1878 and restored by volunteers in 1992. In the long winters when the dam was fully used, loggers slabbed up the huge white pine timbers in the forest and hauled them over ice roads on horse-drawn sleds to Round Lake. The sluice was opened in the spring thaw, pushing the logs ahead on their trip to sawmills. The dam site is now listed on the National Register of Historic Places.

The sluggish south fork of the Flambeau River, which rises in the Round-Pike Lake chain, makes for excellent canoeing and fishing for pike and bass. There are plenty of primitive and abandoned logging roads in the neighborhood, along with the remains of a dam built in the late 1870s. Flynn Lake is also ready to be hiked, with many old lumber roads available for walking. Most are too overgrown for driving. No special permits are necessary to enter either area, both of which are used by naturalists, botanists, wildlife experts, and environmentalists collecting data.

WHISPERS OF CLARK COUNTY

The first time I visited the Highground Veterans Memorial was in the early 1990s, as a midday autumn drizzle spat down from the gunmetal skies. Seen from along the rush of U.S. Highway 10, Neillsville's brick and limestone shoulders were drawn together, as the Clark County seat tried to keep free of the dampness.

I parked the car and walked through the rain along a wide arcade that led directly to a cluster of convoluted bronze figures at a salient of the Vietnam Veterans Memorial. The tinkling of wind chimes from hundreds of bamboo-shaped bronze rods to the rear of the statue made a gentle concert on a dull, gray afternoon. *Fragments*, the life-sized sculpture by artist Robert Kanyusik, dominates the memorial's plaza, with its four supporting figures on a representation of a Native American burial mound. The statue features a helmeted nurse standing protectively over a wounded soldier and two buddies pulling him to safety. The chimes are under the nurse's poncho, each rod inscribed with the names of Wisconsin's 1,132 Vietnam War dead.

Below the ridge, an earthen peace dove effigy edges against a thick woodlot. The mound, with earth from all the state's counties, was built as a living memorial to prisoners of war and those missing in action. It is also meant as a place for those who, while home in body, are missing in spirit.

A National Native American Vietnam Veterans Memorial consists of a ten-ton piece of red granite as the marker base, topped by a Native American soldier in jungle fatigues who is holding a rifle and a staff adorned with eagle feathers. The names of Native soldiers who died in Vietnam are etched into a black granite base that rims the statue.

The addition of new monuments have broadened the Highground scope to include memorials for troops of World Wars I and II, for women veterans, and for families of service personnel. Eventually, markers for the Korean and Gulf Wars will be added.

The Highground is a reflective, but not a mournful, place. Its mission is to honor courage and sacrifice, without either denying or glorifying the pain and suffering of war. This is the wonder of the memorial. Whenever I am in the vicinity, I stop here for

THE ROUTE

Drive west about four miles from the Clark County seat of Neillsville via U.S. Highway 10 to get to the Highground Veterans Memorial. From the Highground, continue on 10 to Rustic Road 76 (Columbia Road). Follow the Rustic Road signage as it traverses several narrow country roads to intersect with County Road B. Take B north to reconnect with U.S. 10.

It [the dove effigy] is a spiritual place where you can go and let your mother, the Earth, hold you. Let the children play on it. Dance on it. Use it to unload your grief and pain, to renew and strengthen you. Lay back in the soft fold of its wings and let Mother Earth unburden you. Then get up and leave your troubles and cares there on the mound, as you walk away, renewed and refreshed.
—Vietnam War veteran John Beaudin (Wa Kanja Hoohega) speaking at the 1989 dedication of the Peace Dove Effigy Mound

Clockwise from Left:
The Woman's Memorial, the National Native American Vietnam Veterans Memorial, and the Vietnam Veterans Memorial stand at the Highground in Neillsville.

James Schmidt and his sons Andy, 6, and Derek, 4, fish on Snyder Lake, just west of Neillsville off of U.S. Highway 10.

TAKE THE RURAL WAY

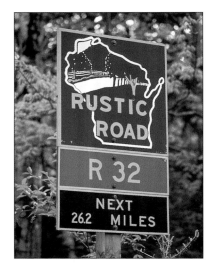

SIGNS PROMINENTLY MARK THE ROUTES OF WISCONSIN'S RUSTIC ROAD SYSTEM.

Wisconsin's Rustic Roads system was created in 1973 when the state legislature promoted the preservation of remaining scenic, lightly traveled roads for the enjoyment of motorists, cyclists, and hikers. To qualify for the program, a road must have such features as rugged landscape, native vegetation and wildlife, or open areas with vistas that make the views unique. A Rustic Road can be dirt, gravel, or paved, but not scheduled for any new construction or widening. It has to be at least two miles long and have a maximum speed of 45 mph.

Yellow and brown signs mark the numbered, officially designated routes. To avoid confusion with the state trunk highway system, the letter "R" is used as a prefix with each number, such as R-76 or R-18.

A ten-member board is responsible for overseeing the system and approving the Rustic Road designation. Those on the panel represent a broad base of Wisconsinites in business, agriculture, tourism, government, utilities, and the general public. There are more than ninety roads in the system, extending about 480 miles in different parts of the state. Each has its own history and scenery.

For more information about Wisconsin's Rustic Roads, contact the Wisconsin Department of Transportation, Box 7913, Madison, WI, 53707-7913; (608) 266-0639.

a few refreshing minutes to reflect on whatever is scooting though my mind. I don't always find answers, but the questions don't seem so large after stopping here.

When leaving the memorial, drive out of the 140-acre park and take in some of the surrounding, low-lying countryside of Clark County. Spooner Creek, an off-again-on-again shallow waterway that merges with the slow-moving Black River, flows between Neillsville and the veterans memorial.

Clark County has 590 miles of streams that meander through three major river basins, with Dickison Creek—in the northwest section of the county—earning bragging rights as the best trout stream around these parts. Waterfowl habitat is also well protected here, with one of the most accessible locales for bird watchers along Sportsman's Lake and Brick Creek, north of Owen. Bring binoculars for close ups.

The two Clark County state-designated Rustic Roads are short, sweet, and relaxing. Rustic Road 73 comprises Robin Road and Cloverdale Avenue, beginning at the intersection of County Road N and Robin. It then edges south to Cloverdale where it runs west to join County Road P, a jaunt of only 2.5 miles. Within that short span are dairy farms, a buffalo-breeding ranch, and a one-lane wooden bridge, which is found on Robin Avenue, spanning the Wisconsin Central railroad tracks. Watch out for the possibility of Amish buggies on this scenic byway.

Rustic Road 76, which is just west of the veterans memorial, is our route. It cuts through the some of the country's heaviest forestland—along Columbia Avenue, Middle Road, Fisher Avenue, Sand Road, and Bruce Mound Avenue between Highway 10 and County Road B. There are plenty of deer to spot, and sandhill cranes often stalk through the fields. Bald eagles are also sometimes seen here, as are numerous species of songbirds that add to the area's natural choir.

Clark County has historically cared about its forests, establishing protected land as early as 1934. Its spread of government-managed woodland now covers nearly 133,000 acres where hunters, hikers, and off-road users can observe the occasional bear, as well as turkeys and grouse. That seems to be the ongoing sense and sensibility of Clark County: healing, preserving, and bringing together—whether by visiting the Highground or simply walking through the quiet woods. If you listen hard enough, there may be some answers in the wind.

LAURA INGALLS WILDER COUNTRY

The early morning sun crawls up slowly from the eastern horizon—within minutes, the rays paint the oaks in a blaze of dawn gold. An osprey screams overhead while Warrentown Coulee is still thick with shadow on its near slopes. Thickets of blackberry bushes—near lightning-shattered, lonely maples—line the ragged barbed wire fence lines that crisscross the valley fields.

This trip begins at Ellsworth, the county seat of Pierce County and the official "Cheese Curd Capital of Wisconsin"—so decreed by Governor Anthony Earl in 1984. The Ellsworth Co-operative Creamery, which opened in 1908, still utilizes 1.5 million pounds of milk to produce rich butter, fabulously squeaky curds, and creamy whey powder. The creamery's four cheese makers work round-the-clock, six days a week to make thirty-three million pounds of cheese every year.

Close to the place where County Road A meets the Great River Road, the Mississippi River widens gently at Lake Pepin, an area rich in game and fish. Nearby Maiden Rock was named to honor the legend of a distraught Native American girl who plunged to her death from the nearby bluffs after being forced to consider marriage to a man she didn't love.

County Road AA, which is barely a quarter-mile north of the border with Pepin County, is a pleasant drive leading to Rustic Road 51, also called 20th Avenue. The scenic artery, a 4.3-mile run through cornfields and thick groves of basswood, maple, butternut, ash, and oak, plugs along eastward until it reaches County Road CC. It crosses a trout stream about midway along the route and then passes a century-plus old church at the junction with CC.

Turn south on CC and follow the road to a three-acre park where a log cabin replica marks the homesite of author Laura Ingalls Wilder, whose stories have delighted readers for generations. Her tales led to a

THE ROUTE

Beginning in Ellsworth, take U.S. Highway 10 east to County Road A. Drive south on A to connect with Wisconsin Highway 35 and continue south to Pierce County Road AA, following Rustic Road 51 (20th Avenue) to the junction of County Road CC. Turn south on CC and drive about three miles to the birthplace of Laura Ingalls Wilder. From there, take CC north to County Road S, which runs northeast to Plum City and continues on to Elmwood. Follow Wisconsin Highway 128 north, and turn west on County Road B into Spring Valley. From there, motor west on Wisconsin Highway 29 to River Falls.

ABOVE:
A STREAM FLOWS LITERALLY ACROSS RUSTIC ROAD 51.
ALTHOUGH THIS ROAD IS NEAR MAIDEN ROCK AND THE
MISSISSIPPI RIVER, IT FEELS FAR OFF THE BEATEN TRACK.

RIGHT:
A TROUT STREAM MEANDERS THROUGH THE WOODS NEAR
PIERCE COUNTY'S RUSTIC ROAD 51.

QUINTESSENTIAL WISCONSIN: CORN GROWS NEAR A TOWN CALLED CREAM.

LEFT:

A SIGN MARKS THE LAURA INGALLS WILDER HISTORICAL SITE.

long-running television program called *Little House on the Prairie* that ran from 1974 to 1983, luring even more readers to Wilder's wonderful collection.

After leaving her homestead, you can divert from our route to explore the coulee country around Pepin. Drive back on CC to Pepin County J, turn left on J and travel through Stockholm. The riverside village was founded in 1853, making it the oldest Swedish settlement in this part of the state. Highway 35 runs through Stockholm if you wish to continue driving south along the Mississippi.

Our trip runs from the Wilder homesite back into Pierce County along CC and S to Plum City. Spin around Nugget Lake Park, four miles north of Plum City, which consists of 752 acres of woods and fields. The 116-acre Nugget Lake is noted for fat bass and hungry crappies.

Continuing along County Road S will lead directly to Elmwood, founded as a logging center in the 1870s. The village's main claims to fame, however, were the numerous UFO sightings in the 1970s that attracted flying saucer aficionados from around the world, although no alien ever presented itself.

Follow Wisconsin Highway 128 and County Road B to Spring Valley, which is halfway between Minneapolis–St. Paul, Minnesota, and Eau Claire, Wisconsin. The discovery of iron in the region in the early 1890s opened the whole valley to business. The town, with its resident population of 1,100, is only six miles south of Interstate 94. Spring Valley is located on the Eau Galle River and has the distinction of being one of the most flooded communities in Wisconsin, calling itself "The Town that Couldn't Be

LAURA INGALLS WILDER KNEW THE FRONTIER

Novelist Laura Ingalls Wilder was born February 7, 1867, in the Chippewa River valley area of Wisconsin—the "big woods" of her stories. Her family had migrated to the Midwest from New England in the 1850s, eventually winding up in Pepin County in 1863.

When Laura began writing in 1930—aided by her daughter, Rose—she described many of her youthful experiences on the family farm in *Little House in the Big Woods.* Her more vivid stories told of hog butchering, baking bread, and collecting maple sap to make syrup. In *Farmer Boy,* she detailed the growing-up years of Almanzo Wilder, a childhood sweetheart who she went on to marry in 1885. The writing career that made her famous and her prodigious creative output finally began winding down when Wilder was seventy-six. She died on February 10, 1957, three days after her ninetieth birthday.

In her honor, each September the town of Pepin celebrates Laura Ingalls Wilder Days with a pancake breakfast and Laura lookalike contests for eight- to ten-year-old girls.

Licked." Major washouts occurred in 1894, 1896, 1903, 1907, 1934, 1938, and 1942. After all this, the locals figured it was damn time to build a dam . . . or relocate the town. The Spring Valley fathers went to the Army Corps of Engineers to seek a flood plain plan. Yet, it took another twenty years before the current rolled-earth, rock-filled dam was approved and built, and finally completed in 1968. The resulting 150-acre Eau Galle Lake and surrounding parkland now attracts upwards of 250,000 people a year.

From Spring Valley, drive west on Wisconsin Highway 29 to River Falls, which was founded by Mexican War veteran Joe Foster, who built a log cabin here alongside the Kinnickinnic River in the winter of 1848. More than a century and a half later, the Kansas City Chiefs hold summer football training camp at the University of Wisconsin–River Falls, a college known for its rough-riding rodeo team.

The Kinnickinnic River in this region is noted for its trout fishing, earning a Class One listing for its population of browns, which make up about 70 percent of the trout population in the river. The river links with the St. Croix National Scenic Riverway at Kinnickinnic State Park. Within the park boundaries, there is a great overlook for camera buffs hoping for that award-winning photo of fog drifting through the valley on a fresh summer morning.

ST. CROIX FALLS

In the late 1800s, western Wisconsin still had a frontier mentality. It was rugged in its geology, with edgy social mores, an on-the-edge life ethos, and raw emotions drawn to the surface by harsh winters, isolation, rocky soil, backbreaking mortgages, and pre-dawn to after-dusk toil. Dodge City had nothing on the towns born amid the thick forests that blanketed Burnett, Polk, Barron, Dunn, Washburn, and St. Croix Counties. By the mid-nineteenth century, after the beaver were depleted by trappers along the St. Croix River, logging took over in its economic place. All the deeper waterways in western Wisconsin became packed with harvested timber on the way to downstream mills. Sometimes, the logs jammed in the narrows and lumberjacks had to climb aboard them to pry loose the deadly thickenings.

Today, tourist brochures tell of snowmobile excursions, waterslide parks, canoe rentals, and resort swimming pools in this area of western Wisconsin, yet you can still get a small taste of the old days on the St. Croix National Scenic Riverway, which includes the St. Croix and Namekagon Rivers. This wilderness retains its untamed liveliness along the 252-mile riverway that has been preserved by the National Wild and Scenic Rivers System since 1968.

At first glance, much of the landscape leading to the riverway is flat (blame the glaciers), but the closer you get to the St. Croix River, the more challenging the terrain becomes. U.S. Highway 53, running south from

THE ROUTE

From St. Croix Falls, take U.S. Highway 8 east to County Road H. Drive south on H to Mains Crossing Road to explore Rustic Road 28. Return to U.S. 8 and travel east to the intersection with U.S. Highway 63 at Turtle Lake. From there, drive north on Rustic Road 67.

The Summit Rock Trail edges through Interstate Park.

This view of the St. Croix National Scenic Riverway is seen from Summit Peak at Interstate Park in St. Croix Falls.

Superior to Eau Claire, forms the eastern border of this recreational area, while the Minnesota state line makes the western border. On the north, the boundary is Wisconsin Highway 77, while the southern perimeter is Interstate 94.

The Upper St. Croix and the Namekagon offer about two hundred miles of canoeable water. The Namekagon begins as a pencil-thin trout stream at Namekagon Lake Dam at the southern tip of the Chequamegon National Forest of Bayfield County. It flows ninety-eight miles south to meet the St. Croix, through second-growth woods, meadowland, and marsh. Lofty sandbanks are found around sharp bends, with portages required at the Pacwawong, Phipps, and Trego dams. Several landings present camping opportunities—a visitor center is available for details at the U.S. Highway 53 bridge over the Namekagon in the village of Trego.

The Upper St. Croix starts as a spring behind the Gordon Dam in Douglas County and then becomes the western perimeter of Wisconsin, running deeper and faster after it links with the Namekagon. The St. Croix flows south for 102 miles to plunge over the sixty-foot-high hydroelectric dam at the Badger State city of St. Croix Falls.

On its way south, the St. Croix hosts two Minnesota state parks and two state forests on the Minnesota side, with the Crex Meadows, Fish Lake wildlife areas, and the Governor Knowles State Forest among the top natural attractions on the Wisconsin bank. Interstate Park, of St. Croix Falls, became one of Wisconsin's first state parks when, in 1878, fifty thousand acres of public land—scattered timberlands around Lincoln, Iron, Vilas, and Oneida Counties—were set aside by the state legislature for potential future use. In 1895, locals' hard-fought efforts convinced the Wisconsin legislature to approve a commission to develop Interstate Park at St. Croix Falls. The first section of land was acquired in 1900, setting the stage for the state's extensive state park system today.

The Lower St. Croix runs fifty-two miles from the St. Croix Falls Dam southward to Prescott, Wisconsin, where it flows into the Mississippi River. The most picturesque part of this lower section are the Dalles just south of St. Croix Falls, where the river speeds up over a two-mile stretch, racing along at a seventy- to one-hundred-foot depths between the lofty gorges. After the river flows away from the Dalles, it spreads out and becomes shallow again while traveling between high banks over the next twenty miles. At Hudson, Wisconsin, the river widens, reaching 7,400 feet across.

Backroads here make for interesting driving. One such jaunt is the gravely Rustic Road 28, or Mains Crossing Road, which is about twelve miles east of St. Croix Falls on U.S. Highway 8/Wisconsin Highway 46. The scenic drive, about a half mile south of 8/46, is a 5.2-mile run between Polk County Roads H on the west and D on the east. Starting at County H (110th Street), you'll spot the trim Balsam Lutheran Church at the crest of a hill, with Apple River County Park on the right. The up-and-down road crosses the river via an old stone bridge. The Apple River Town Hall is midway along the route with a rare round barn down the road. This route ends at the Joel Marsh State Wildlife Area, so turn north on County Road JJ to reconnect with U.S. 8.

Rustic Road 67 (Old County Line Street) is an additional worthy byway. The gravel road is 4.6 miles long, and can be picked up next to tiny Elbow Lake, just off of the intersection of U.S. 8 and U.S. 63. The Canyon Road Inn, a bed and breakfast, is found along this winding gravel road. It is a neat guesthouse run by Ken and Judy Ahlberg who purchased it in 1998. Old County Line Street rides the Polk and Barron County border north to 160th Avenue, which runs east to U.S. 63.

Another backcountry drive worth noting in Polk County is Rustic Road 41 on Hunky Dory Road (also known as 70th Street). The route is just off of County Road E, south of Big Round Lake, and can be reached by driving north on County Road D from U.S. 8. The gravel road passes woods and deep gullies to link with Clara Lake Road where the Hunky Dory Resort can be found. The camp has been popular since it opened in the late nineteenth century.

An alternate drive in adjacent Barron County—where it abuts Washburn County on the north— can be reached by driving east on U.S. 8 to Barron, then north on Highway 25 to 24th Avenue. Motor east on 24th to County Road V (16th Avenue), turn north and continue on V. This route melds with Rustic Road 83 (13¾-16th Street) and runs to 30th Avenue, which is the border road between Barron and Washburn Counties. This drive is particularly nice in the autumn when the sumac flashes its deep crimson and the poplar groves shimmy in the breeze. As you cross the county border, you have the option to continue on County V past the Bear Lake State Wildlife Area and link with U.S. 63 at Shell Lake to the north, or turn west on 30th Avenue where you'll meet 63 at Barronett. Whichever road you choose to take can be called the "less traveled," and it's there that you'll find your own adventure.

LUMBERMEN DRIVE LOGS OVER THE APPLE RIVER FALLS IN THIS PHOTOGRAPH FROM 1860. (MINNESOTA HISTORICAL SOCIETY)

PART II

THE NORTHEAST: NATURAL WONDERS AND BACKROAD TREASURES

TREES LINE SCOTT LAKE ROAD IN THE NICOLET NATIONAL FOREST.

HOLLY COHN WALKS ALONG COUNTY ROAD K NEAR LITTLE STAR LAKE.

Northeastern Wisconsin has just about everything one needs for an abundance of quality getaway time—camping, hiking, fishing, and more. Just ask the locals, whose promotional enthusiasm is clearly heartfelt.

From the art galleries and farmers' markets of Door County to the Heritage Scenic Byways of the Nicolet National Forest, the region is made for vacations and backcountry driving. This is a land where tree-canopied roads in the Northern Highland–American Legion State Forest put European cathedrals to shame; where a late summer Egg Harbor fish boil rivals a gourmet spread of five-star delectables; where a full-rigged schooner sailing off Sturgeon Bay tops a cruise ship on the lively Caribbean. The blackberries here are blacker, the whitetails swifter, the eagles more stately, and the campgrounds more inviting.

Come to the Northeast to see all this wonderment firsthand and encourage the year-round residents to tell you the secrets of the area. They insist that the lakes are clearer and deeper here and contain more walleyes than almost any other section of the state. Of course, all these claims are easily taken to task by just-as-proud Wisconsinites from other parts of the state, but Northeasterners have good reason to take pride in their region.

To find this "bit o' heaven," drive to where the state snuggles up to the southern border of Michigan's Upper Peninsula. Vilas, Forest, Oneida, and adjacent border counties sprawl over vast tracts of woodland that have rebounded from logging era devastation. With careful nurturing by the state and federal forest service workers, northeastern Wisconsin has come into its own as a popular vacation spot with much to offer.

NORTHERN HIGHLAND– AMERICAN LEGION STATE FOREST

THE ROUTE

Beginning at Phelps, take County Road K west to Star Lake. Continue west on K from Star Lake to County Road M— this stretch of the trip is also designated as Rustic Road 60. Follow County K/M north to Boulder Junction; then continue west on K and jog south on County Road W to Manitowish Waters.

Trees, trees, trees. The old saw not withstanding, the Northern Highland–American Legion State Forest is one place in Wisconsin where you can still see the forest for the trees. For a premier way to see what the forest has to offer, take County Road K, one of a spiderweb of backcountry roads that meander through these thick, mostly second-growth woods.

This 222,000-acre property sprawls across parts of Vilas, Oneida and Iron Counties, making it the largest single piece of land owned by Wisconsin. Together, Wisconsin's northern state forests—the Northern Highland–American Legion, Black River, Brule River, Flambeau River, and Governor Knowles—make up more than 428,000 acres.

Glaciers formed this corner of Wisconsin ten thousand years ago, untidy as toddlers as they dumped rocks all over the region. As the debris from the glaciers was slowly covered with thin soil, the rocky ridges became today's Northern Highland forested hills. Many of the shallow glacial lakes have evolved into the bogs that can be found around almost every turn.

ABOVE, TOP:
A PILEATED WOODPECKER DRILLS FOR INSECTS.

ABOVE, CENTER:
A BUTTERFLY LIGHTS ON A FLOWER IN THE WOODS ALONG COUNTY ROAD K.

ABOVE, BOTTOM:
THIS WEATHERED SIGN STANDS OUTSIDE A ONCE-POPULAR BAIT SHOP, NOW CLOSED. THE TINY STORE HAD BEEN RUN BY TWO
SISTERS WHO WERE LONGTIME RESIDENTS OF THE AREA.

A SECTION OF COUNTY ROAD K HAS BEEN DESIGNATED AS WISCONSIN'S RUSTIC ROAD 60. IF ONE JUDGED IT ON SCENIC BEAUTY
ALONE, IT COULD WELL BE THE BEST IN WISCONSIN'S RUSTIC ROAD SYSTEM.

More than nine hundred lakes are within the 527-square-mile exterior boundary of Northern Highland–American Legion, ranging from small, unnamed lakes to the 4,000-acre Trout Lake. There are also 247 miles of waterways within the forest boundaries, which makes it the greatest concentration of fresh water in the state. As such, water recreation is a prime draw for the two million visitors a year who come to the region.

The original road builders of the Northern Highland region had to loop around the area's numerous bodies of water, fill in damp, low-lying depressions, push up wooded hills, and generally sweat their way through the tangled black raspberry and chokecherry brush to achieve each mile. Early surveyors plowed through this neck of the untracked woods in the mid 1800s. Today, a Global Positioning System unit is used to accurately locate and map trails, rivers, lakes, and other features in the forest that need identification.

In 1925, Northern Highland–American Legion was established by the state around the headwaters of the rivers that sprang out of the granite landscape along the Wisconsin-Michigan border. It has remained a prime tourist attraction, with more than nine hundred campsites and two outdoor group camps able to accommodate a total of one hundred outdoors fans. Boat landings are provided at most campgrounds, and winter camping is permitted at the Clear Lake site. The forest also has eight picnic areas with drinking water and toilets, as well as many wayside picnic sites.

Star Lake is midway between Conover and Boulder Junction on County K. Ninety percent of the 1,200-acre lake's shoreline is state owned. Bill Hintz's historical Star Lake Lodge and Resort, which was originally developed in 1894 as the Waldheim Hotel, is typical of recreational facilities along the lake. The resort was renovated after World War II, with indoor flush toilets installed in 1945, and went through several owners before being purchased by the Hintzes in 1980. Renovation has continued over the past few years, yet the Star Lake Lodge still retains all the necessary woodsy charm one would expect.

Roughing it is also possible within the forest. Crystal Lake, Muskie Lake, Clear Lake, and Firefly Lake accept reservations from campers, and wilderness camping is available for backpackers year around.

Hikers can find a range of challenges in the Northern Highland–American Legion Forest. The 12.5-mile-long Lumberjack Trail near Boulder Junction, with grass and dirt pathways, is easily walked, but the hilly Fallison Trail—reached by driving south on County M from Boulder Junction—has at least one strenuous loop. For kids, the two legs of the Star Lake Nature and Hiking Trail are ideal. They are located on the north side of Star Lake and are easily accessible off County K along Statehouse Road, past the West Star Lake Campground. Parking is available at the trailhead, which includes a mile-long nature interpretive trail and a 2.5-mile-long hiking trail that the smaller fry can also enjoy.

The best bike path in the region is the Bearskin State Trail, which stretches for eighteen miles between Minocqua, at the far southern tip of the state forest, and Oneida County's Road K. The trail parallels the low marshlands of Bearskin Creek—crossing the waterway at least nine times—and traverses the channel between Lakes Kawaguesaga and Minocqua. The trail was built on an old railroad grade, purchased by the state in 1973, and has a crushed granite surface that provides smooth sailing—even for tykes on bikes.

Friends have said that the canoeing in the Northern Highland is among the best in Wisconsin, especially along the Manitowish River as it drifts forty-four miles from High Lake to the Flambeau Flowage. One recommended put-in site is the High Lake boat landing on the south side of County B, where a small stream meanders turtle-like to the lake. Paddle southwest through a culvert into Fishtrap Lake, which then opens a route past Johnson and Nixon Creeks. Pull out upstream from the Fishtrap Dam. Another good route is the flowage from Fishtrap Dam to County K. To find a viable launch site, take County M north from Boulder Junction to meet High-Fishtrap Road. Stay on the right, which is Dam Road, and put in downstream from the boat landing there.

Wisconsin has a history of caring for its waterways and the creatures that inhabit them. It is the only state in the nation with research data on fisheries that extends back to 1946, allowing scientists access to excellent long-term material for study. Five lakes in the Northern Highland Forest are managed by the state to evaluate the feeding habits, reproduction, stocking, and other details concerning fish.

You can often watch the state workers on Escanaba, Pallette, Nebish, Spruce, and Mystery Lakes as they go about their tasks tagging and recording. The major research station on Escanaba Lake is 3.5 miles from any paved road, deep in the heart of the forest. You can help researchers by registering to fish at any one of the five lakes in their study. Along with a regular fishing license, you need a permit purchased from participating stores around Vilas County or at area DNR offices. The permit is returned to state biologists after they examine your catch—and there's nothing fishy about it at all.

THE GANGSTERS OF MANITOWISH WATERS

Al Capone slept here. John Dillinger vacationed there. Baby Face Nelson ate over there.

The North Woods of the 1930s were busy when it came to bootleggers and B-role mobsters. If local legends are true from Trout Lake to the St. Croix Flowage, there must have been more gangsters per acre than white-tailed deer up here when Prohibition was in flower.

The bad guys headed toward Manitowish Waters from Chicago or the Twin Cities to escape the heat of the city concrete and the coppers hot on their trails. The press of the day was not far behind, as they slavishly followed the derring-do of the bank robbers and murderers.

THE ROUTE

To reach Manitowish Waters from Rhinelander, take Wisconsin Highway 47 north and west to Woodruff, then follow U.S. Highway 51 north. From Manitowish Waters, follow County Road W north and east to Presque Isle.

THE LAST GLOW FROM THE DAY'S SUNLIGHT CATCHES A GREAT BLUE HERON STALKING ALONG THE SHORE AT MEMORIAL PARK IN PRESQUE ISLE.

LITTLE BOHEMIA, A FORMER RESORT, IS NOW A RESTAURANT.

THE BULLET HOLES FROM JOHN DILLINGER'S FAMOUS SHOOT-OUT WITH POLICE HAVE BEEN LEFT IN THE WINDOWS OF LITTLE BOHEMIA.

A WANTED POSTER AND OTHER MEMO-RABILIA FROM THE DAYS OF JOHN DILLINGER ARE ON DISPLAY AT LITTLE BOHEMIA.

All through the Midwest, these characters skirted the fringes of society to rob and shoot their way into infamy. And it really was hard work— all that leaping over bank tellers' counters to grab fistfuls of greenbacks— so it was only natural to feel the urge to get away from it all for a time. They headed north along U.S. Highway 51, just as tourists do today on pleasant vacation afternoons.

The more well-off gangsters, such as Al Capone, had their personal, private retreats well off the beaten path. Scarface and pals motored to Couderay, a hamlet in northwestern Wisconsin, where they had a complex called "The Hideout." The complex of squat stone buildings is now a steakhouse, reached off Sawyer County Road CC, a couple of miles north of Wisconsin Highway 70, near what is now the Lac Courte Oreilles Indian Reservation. Whenever they drove into town, the locals gave them a respectfully wide berth.

Other thugs were not lucky enough to have such luxurious accommodations—they just needed a hole in which to hide. Early in the spring of 1934, John Dillinger broke out of an "escape proof jail" in Indiana. On April 12, after the escape, he and several of his men robbed the Warsaw, Indiana, police station and ran off with two revolvers, several bulletproof vests, and a sheriff's squad car. They drove across the Illinois border to hide out in Chicago, but their interstate crime quickly grabbed the attention of the Windy City's FBI office and J. Edgar Hoover himself.

Dillinger figured it was time to bolt for Wisconsin. On April 20, he and his men packed clean underwear, fresh ammunition, and their toothbrushes, and convoyed north to Vilas County, Wisconsin, in three cars. Their destination was a small resort on Little Star Lake called Little Bohemia, operated by Emil Wanatka. The resort owner—not knowing the real identity of his guests—sat down with the vacationers for a friendly game of cards after dinner. He soon noticed with alarm that his newly arrived visitors were well armed—shoulder holsters bulging with firepower.

Wanatka naturally worried that anything could happen with such a crowd on hand, which included the notorious Lester Gillis (a.k.a. Baby Face Nelson), a psychopathic killer. Subsequently, despite being closely watched, Wanatka's wife smuggled out a note for help. The sheriff, when alerted, realized that any showdown with such dangerous desperadoes was well beyond his scope, so he contacted the FBI, who immediately promised aid. Feds from St. Paul and Chicago flew to Rhinelander, the closest airport to Little Bohemia, where they joined local police.

The government force headed toward Little Bohemia, bouncing over the rough dirt roads in the late spring cold. Two of their five cars broke down and eight agents had to ride most of the freezing way perched on the running boards of the other cars. According to the plan, agents would storm the front door of the lodge, with other officers flanking the structure on the right and left sides. Since the resort was on a steep slope leading to the water, they figured that way was blocked. But no one had told the force about the resort's two watchdogs, and the animals began barking as soon as the agents drove up.

In the resulting confusion, several locals who had been drinking in the resort bar left the building and walked to their car. The cold and tired agents in the damp woods thought that the gangsters were leaving. They opened fire, killing one innocent man in the hail of bullets and seriously wounding two others.

Alarmed by the gunfire, the Dillinger gang ran out the back door toward the night-black lake. Agents chasing them either fell into a hidden drainage ditch or became tangled in a barbed wire fence that ran along the property line. In an ensuing gunfight between Baby Face Nelson and a posse of several agents aided by a town constable, one federal officer was killed and two others wounded. All the gang got away. Dillinger and two of his men commandeered a car in nearby Park Falls and headed toward St. Paul, eventually rerouting their trip to return to Chicago. A few months later, Dillinger was shot to death outside a movie theater in Chicago.

Years after the incident, Little Bohemia has the same feel as it did in old newspaper photos—small porch in front, tiny overnight cabins scattered around the fringes of the dark brown main building, lake lapping quietly in the background, bullet holes still pockmarking the walls and windows.

After leaving the Little Bohemia grounds, I follow Vilas County Road W north and east toward Presque Isle, passing a kitchen design center, a gift shop, and a drive-up bank in a little shopping mall adjacent to an IGA grocery store. Cranberry Collectibles and the Village Soda Grill are shuttered for the evening. Things are slow tonight at the Bavarian Inn and few lights are on in the Pea Patch Motel. As I look down the street at the small-town bank and the collectibles shop filled with treasures, I wonder what John Dillinger would have thought of it all.

"Hmm . . . that bank. . . ."

NICOLET NATIONAL FOREST

It's not winter yet, but there is a touch of nose-numbing frost hovering on autumn's cool breath as I roll along Wisconsin Highway 70, whizzing eastward from robust Eagle River, the snowmobile capital of northern Wisconsin. Within minutes beyond the town, spruce-shrouded Vilas County is in my rearview mirror and Forest County stretches out ahead.

The county, which rubs shoulders with the rock-ribbed Upper Peninsula of Michigan, is the primary home to the Nicolet National Forest. Nicolet covers nearly 661,400 acres in Forest, Florence, Langlade, Oconto, Oneida, and Vilas Counties. It has a rich history and has been inhabited by humans for at least ten thousand years. In 1634, French explorer and fur trader, Jean Nicolet—for whom the forest is named—was the first European to wander through the area.

Following hard on the heels of the fur trade, a burgeoning lumber industry was established by the mid 1800s—with loggers making quick work of the ancient trees. When the lumber ran out in the 1920s, a flood

THE ROUTE

Beginning at Eagle River, follow Wisconsin Highway 70 east to Fishel Road. From there, drive along Rustic Road 34, which leads to Alvin.

LEAVES FALL ON MILITARY ROAD IN THE NICOLET NATIONAL FOREST.

THE LAST FEW LEAVES OF AUTUMN DANGLE FROM BRANCHES ALONG SCOTT LAKE ROAD IN THE NICOLET NATIONAL FOREST.

of immigrant farmers tried their luck blowing out stumps to clear fields for planting. It wasn't long before they realized that the soil would not support their crops. The land lay abandoned until the late 1920s when the federal government started buying tax-delinquent property with the idea of someday establishing a national forest. In 1929, a Forest Service office was set up in Park Falls to keep an eye on the acquisitions.

President Herbert Hoover finally established the Nicolet National Forest in March 1933, with headquarters in Park Falls and a second office in Rhinelander. Although originally a part of the Nicolet unit, the Chequamegon, Wisconsin's other national forest, was set up as a separate unit in November 1933, by President Franklin Roosevelt. When the Depression tossed hundreds of thousands of workers off the job, many joined the Civilian Conservation Corps, which planted acres of red pine, constructed fire lanes, and made recreational facilities throughout the government land. In the mid 1980s, a land plan was developed for both the Chequamegon and the Nicolet. Over the next decade, the project was revised and strengthened to produce a joint proposal for accommodating the economic, environmental, and recreational needs for the combined Chequamegon-Nicolet National Forests.

The Nicolet's Forest County is easy to traverse, with an excellent combination of state and local roadways. Its topography covers 1,041 craggy square miles, of which 59 percent are public lands, with 84 percent being stands of aspen, spruce, red pine, and other tree varieties. There are 824 lakes within the county, giving it the sixth highest number of lakes in the state. Forest is sparsely populated. Only about ten thousand people live in the county, averaging only nine folks per square mile, so the roads can be empty—stretching to the horizon with no sign of life for miles.

Yet there are bright lights—neon, in fact. The Northern Lights Casino/Potawatomi Bingo on Wisconsin Highway 32 in Carter and the Mole Lake Casino in the southwest corner of Forest County are the county's two largest employers. The favorable economic impact of these operations has helped draw back Native American residents who had left to find jobs elsewhere.

The Forest County Potawatomi reservation holdings are a checkerboard of twelve thousand acres. The tribe operates a medical center and the Indian Springs Lodge and Convention Center in Carter, located in the far southern section of Forest County along Highway 32. North of Wabeno on County Road H is the Potawatomi Red Deer Ranch, which sells meat to restaurants around the country, as well as the tribe's casino and bingo hall in Milwaukee. The Potawatomi tribe now employs 520 people in Forest County and about 1,500 in Milwaukee. With the growth of the casinos and related businesses, unemployment within the tribe has dropped to approximately 25 percent, down from 90 percent about a decade ago.

The Sokaogon (Mole Lake) Band of Lake Superior Chippewa live on a reservation near Crandon. The tribal members regularly harvest wild rice from Rice Lake, one of the few remaining natural beds of the nut-brown rice in Wisconsin. Their legends tell how early Chippewa clans migrated a thousand years ago from Canada to Madeline Island in Lake Superior off Bayfield County, and that their ancestors were led by visions to a land where food would grow on the water. The Sokaogon ended their journey here, feeling that the wild rice fit their vision quest. *Sokaogon* means "Post in the Lake" people, which some historians believe might have referred to a petrified tree that stood as a silent sentinel of the past in Post Lake—near the current Mole Lake Reservation of Forest County. The tribe is also often referred to as the Lost Tribe, because the deed to its twelve-square-mile reservation was lost in a shipwreck in 1854. After an extended struggle, the Sokaogon were finally noticed by federal authorities and gained reservation status in 1937.

All of this history and legend are out there in Forest County, concealed by the greenery, waiting to be discovered.

To step even closer to that past, a spirit-minded motorist might take Rustic Road 34 as it edges through northern Forest County only four miles from the Wisconsin-Michigan border. Pick up the 8.8-mile sometimes-paved-sometimes-gravel trail from Highway 70 on Fishel Road—following its curving length across the tannin-colored, boulder-bottomed Brule River and the shallow Alvin Creek over to Carey Dam Road. Pause at the waterways for a time and watch the current carry away sticks and leaves, like thoughts on a busy day. Then keep going along Lakeview Drive, on the way past shallow May Lake into the village of Alvin, which perches along the shoulder of Wisconsin Highway 55.

And everywhere are trees, trees, wonderful trees. Obviously, Forest County lives up to its name.

Marinette County Memories

The Peshtigo River current tumbles along as a thundering swirl of brown froth and head-twisting eddies. Rafting the Peshtigo is not a place for the overconfident, because the torrent literally roars through Marinette County's backwoods. Skilled outfitters, such as those at Kosir's Rapid Rafts, match their clients with the appropriate difficulty level of the rapids. For safety, they ensure that shorter, smoother passages are for beginners and reserve the tougher stretches for the more advanced. At the Kosir family raft headquarters in Athelstane, more than one hundred lost shoes are nailed to an outbuilding wall as a tribute to the wild ride. It's a display that owner Mickie Kosir calls "The Lost Soles of the Peshtigo."

Marinette County, about sixty miles north of Green Bay, is all about water and has rightfully earned the tagline "Wisconsin's Waterfall Capital." Rivers and creeks tumble over drops that range from a few feet to twenty or more and careen through narrow canyons, providing admirable photo opportunities.

There are at least a dozen great waterfalls to see in western Marinette County. Veteran's Falls in Veteran's Memorial Park, lies just west of the hamlet of Crivitz on the Thunder River. Down a steep slope leading to the rushing water, you'll find a picturesque little wooden bridge leaping over

THE ROUTE

Take County Road W west from Crivitz to follow Rustic Road 32 (Parkway Road) north. Continue north on Parkway Road to the entrance of Goodman Park.

ABOVE:
THE PESHTIGO RIVER RUSHES THROUGH GOODMAN COUNTY PARK.

LEFT:
VIRTUALLY IN THE MIDDLE OF NOWHERE, A SHRINE HAS BEEN BUILT—COMPLETE WITH MAILBOX—ON BENSON LAKE ROAD.

FACING PAGE:
GOODMAN PARK ROAD OFFERS A PEACEFUL DRIVE.

the falls. Among the most photogenic neighborhoods in Wisconsin's North Country is the area around High Falls Dam, along High Falls Road, which is north off of Parkway Road across from Veteran's Memorial Park. To discover Cauldron Falls Dam, drive along Boat Landing 8 Road off Parkway Road. The dam here creates a 1,200-acre flowage and marshland that is well populated by game fish and migratory waterfowl. McClintock Falls is in McClintock Park farther north on Parkway, with its plunging rapids arched by a series of almost Zen-like bridges. Goodman Park, also along Parkway, is host to Strong Falls.

Waterfall hunting in this county should also include the series of falls near Twelve Foot Falls County Park, which can be reached by driving south on Lily Lake Road from U.S. Highway 8. The area includes the splish-splashing tumble of Bull Falls, Eighteen Foot Falls, Twelve Foot Falls, and Eight Foot Falls. Each offers its own musical stylization to a woodsy, watery symphony.

Other great waterfalls in the county include Long Slide Falls and Smalley Falls on Morgan Park Road east of U.S. Highway 141; Pemene Falls on the Menominee River off of County Road Z; and Dave's Falls— named after a lumberjack who was killed there while unplugging a log jam—south of Amberg on the Pike River. Second-growth forest carpets

QUEEN MARINETTE RULES THE FRONTIER

Marie Chevalier could not read or write but she was a smart, tough businesswoman in a frontier world. Born around 1793 at Post Lake in Wisconsin's far northern woods, Chevalier was the granddaughter of the Great Marten, a local Native American chief, and the daughter of Bartelemi Chevalier, a respected French-Canadian fur trader who had a post in Green Bay.

When she was small, Marie was nicknamed "Marie Antoinette" in honor of her grandmother, who was baptized in the era of the French queen of the same name. It wasn't long before little Marie became known as Queen Marinette, as the "Marie Antoinette" gradually slurred into one word.

In 1800, when she was only fourteen, young Marie married trader John Jacobs and soon had three children. On one expedition into Canada, Jacobs disappeared, so Ms. Chevalier-Jacobs (a.k.a. Queen Marinette) took over total management of the family's trading post operations.

She eventually remarried another trader and had another three youngsters, continuing to oper-

QUEEN MARINETTE'S HOME, PICTURED HERE, WAS ONE OF THE FIRST HOUSES BUILT IN THE TOWN OF MARINETTE. (WISCONSIN HISTORICAL SOCIETY, WHi (X3) 23854)

ate her store on the Wisconsin side of the turbulent Menominee River. Her second husband, William Farnsworth, erected a sawmill and built his wife the first frame house in northeastern Wisconsin. Over the years, other homes and buildings were built nearby. Today, this site is now the city of Marinette, named after this doughty woman, as is the surrounding Marinette County. Queen Marinette died June 3, 1865, and is buried in Green Bay.

The Great Peshtigo Fire

Peshtigo, in southeastern Marinette County, is often dubbed "King of the Boom Towns." It earned its title in the nineteenth century as a fast-growing settlement of loggers, settlers, railroad workers, and eager business folks wishing to set down roots along Wisconsin's resource-rich frontier.

The city gained its place in history during the perilously dry summer of 1871. Sparks from passing trains set the dry weeds ablaze along newly laid railroad tracks, and by early autumn, smoke from fires in the woods hung over the county. On the night of October 8, the horizon was livid with the dull glow of flames, but no one was prepared for the ensuing tragedy.

The bell in St. Mary's Church began to peal frantically around 8:30 P.M., as a watchman sounded the alarm. By 10:00 P.M., a tornado of flame had descended on the town, which burned to the ground in minutes. More than eight hundred people died in the inferno, a hundred times more than in Chicago's legendary fire, which had raged on the same day.

This drawing of the Peshtigo fire appeared in *Harper's Weekly* on November 25, 1871. (Wisconsin Historical Society, WHi (X3) 96)

The Peshtigo Fire Museum, housed in the first church built after the blaze, stands in white simplicity along Oconto Avenue. Every year, the town holds a memorial service for the victims of the 1881 fire and church bells toll. Outside the church museum in the adjacent cemetery, a pathway leads past antiquated marble tombstones and well-worn gray stone monuments to a large grave holding three hundred unidentified victims.

The last human survivor of the great fire died in 1916, but the only building in Peshtigo that remained intact after the blaze remains full of life. The small frame house at 150 South Beele Avenue, now owned by Kathy and Wade Schenk, was under construction at the time of the fire and did not burn, because it was being framed out with fresh, green wood. Today, a clutter of kids' toys is abandoned near the front porch, reminders that young Alycia, Alex, and Andrea Schenk live here now.

"But no, no ghosts are here that we are aware of," says Kathy Schenk.

Perhaps.

---

the landscape around these falls with a surf of green that is cooling to the eyes in the summer.

Delectable Door County

Door County, the thumbnail on the mitten shape of Wisconsin, is ideal for all kinds of transportation—driving, sailing, and walking. A maze of hiking trails winds through county and state parks, and the water of Green Bay and Lake Michigan surrounds the region. Toss in a jumble of art galleries, ice cream parlors, buy-all-you-want farmers' markets, antique shops, and upscale resorts, and it is clear why Door County is a favorite getaway.

The route

From Sturgeon Bay, take Wisconsin Highway 57 north to Baileys Harbor on the Lake Michigan side of the Door County peninsula. Just south of Baileys Harbor, cut across the landscape on County Road E west to Egg Harbor. From there, follow Wisconsin Highway 42 north to Gills Rock to catch the ferry to Washington Island.

ORANGE HAWKWEED GROWS IN
DOOR COUNTY'S WHITEFISH
DUNES STATE PARK.

A WOODEN WALKWAY LEADS TO
RIDGES SANCTUARY.

SHELLS COVER THE BEACH
IN NORTHPORT.

With almost seven miles of shoreline on over 3,700 acres of land, Peninsula State Park is one of the most popular in Wisconsin's impressive system of state parks.

The question for inhabitants of the area today is how to protect the county's remaining open spaces, as well as keep a lid on taxes. The number of farms in the county is decreasing and what often takes their place are vacation homes or shopping malls. Residents are concerned about this rush to build, which threatens much of the original natural landscape.

Potawatomi State Park, in southern Door County, was once going to be a military base, but minds changed, and the 1,200-acre park was developed in 1928. Steep slopes and limestone cliffs rear up from the cold waters of Sturgeon Bay, which opens onto Green Bay off Sherwood Point. Scamper up the park's seventy-four-foot-tall observation tower atop the park's highest bluff for an eye-opening look over the blue-green waters of the bay, 225 feet below.

The city of Sturgeon Bay, located southeast of the park on Wisconsin Highways 42 and 57, is one of the many towns in Door County that are fun to explore. It was settled in 1835 as a lumber town, and today provides treasures like Sunset Park on Bayshore Drive—a neat little spot to relax and think about the past.

For those who want to understand Door County, the Ridges Sanctuary near Baileys Harbor is an open book of geological and botanical history. Over the centuries, Lake Michigan's waves have left a shoreline of hardened sand and exposed rock. Today, these ridges leading up from the water's edge present a washboard feel to the slope. The plants of this area are just as fascinating, with dwarf mistletoe, black spruce, lichens, red pine, balsam fir, and cranberry bushes among the many varieties of the large and the small. The combination of shade, boggy depressions, and sandy soils attract a spread of flora. Northern species of plants remain strong because of the Lake Michigan climate, which combines a cooler spring and summer with a warmer fall and winter.

In the mid 1860s, the United Lighthouse Service began administering the land now occupied by the reserve. The service installed two range lights as navigational aids at the mouth of Baileys Harbor in 1896. In 1937, as commercial shipping to the region decreased, citizen volunteers took over the property and formed the nonprofit Ridges Sanctuary. The site became one of Wisconsin's first state-designated natural areas in 1953. To find the sanctuary, drive along Highway 57 north from the village of Baileys Harbor and turn right on County Road Q, then enter the first driveway on the right. The grounds are open year-round.

Peninsula State Park is one of the most popular parks in Wisconsin, offering an eighteen-hole golf course, boat ramps, picnic areas, tennis courts, snowmobile trails, and a sledding hill. Peninsula spreads its leafy arms along the Green Bay side of the peninsula, located on Highway 42 at the northern edge of Fish Creek. While the park's camping sites are usually booked solid during the summer, you can still find solitude along its nineteen miles of trails.

THIS VINTAGE POSTCARD GUARANTEES THAT WISCONSIN IS "THE NATION'S SUMMER VACATION-LAND WHERE FRIENDS AND NATURE MEET."

Newport State Park is another exceptional place to get in touch with one's natural self. The park is located five miles east of Ellison Bay on Highway 42, then east on County Highway NP. A century ago, there was a village here to service the loggers and lumber freighters. Now, only a few building foundations are reminders of that past life.

Newport allows camping only by backpackers, who hike in from parking lots one- to more-than-three-miles away. The Rowleys Bay/Ridge Trail is one of the longest of the several marked loops where thick stands of maple, beech, and birch trees are impressively tall, allowing only shafts of sun to spotlight the ground cover of lady's-slippers, butter-and-eggs, trillium, and ferns. The trail skirts several of the park's rustic camping sites, with the greatest views along craggy Varney Point.

Gift shops in Sturgeon Bay and other towns like Fish Creek, Ephraim, Egg Harbor, and Sister Bay, can provide the necessary tee shirt or designer baseball cap for a vacation reminder, but Washington Island, north of the Door County mainland, is a part of the county that you won't forget. Escape to the solitude of Washington Island, settled by Icelandic fisherfolk in the late 1800s, and view the works of local artists at the Art and Nature Center, which makes its home in a converted 1904 school building.

On the ferry ride from Gills Rock to Washington Island's harbor, you will pass Plum Island and its historically important lighthouses, keepers' residences, and boathouses. Offshore is the *Porte des Morts,* or "Death's Door," which describes the six-mile-wide passage between Lake Michigan and Green Bay. Throughout history, the swift currents, wave action, and sudden storms have regularly sent ships to their doom. The Door County Maritime Museum in Sturgeon Bay tells many of their stories.

Rock Island, off the far side of Washington Island, may be Wisconsin's most remote state park. French explorer Jean Nicolet landed at Rock Island in August 1634 before moving down on the peninsula south to what today is Sturgeon Bay. Tiny Rock Island, which is barely a mile wide and three-quarters of a mile long, is now a state park with several excellent hiking trails around its perimeter. The island can be reached aboard the Kafi, a ferry that runs from the landing on Washington Island's Indian Point Road to the Thordarson Boat House, for a day of hiking.

Before leaving Door County, be sure to take in at least one fish boil, a Scandinavian tradition whereby water is boiled in an iron pot hanging over an open fire. Inside the kettle, pounds of robust Wisconsin potatoes, onions, and Lake Michigan whitefish froth away. When the concoction is deemed ready, kerosene is poured over the flames, which causes the pot to boil over, removing all the fats. Usually served with fresh corn-on-the-cob and topped off with cherry pie and smooth vanilla ice cream, the meal is fit for a Viking—or a hungry vacationer.

PART III

THE SOUTHWEST:
WISCONSIN'S RIVERLAND

FACING PAGE:
THIS STUNNING VIEW OF THE BAD AX RIVER IS AVAILABLE FROM HECKS POINT ROAD.

ABOVE:
A CRISP FALL MORNING BRINGS FROST TO A FIELD SOUTH OF FOUNTAIN CITY. BEHIND THE BALES OF HAY RISE THE BLUFFS THAT ARE SO COMMON ALONG THE GREAT RIVER ROAD.

The Mississippi River defines the perimeter of southwestern Wisconsin, where limestone hills dangle their chalky toes in the shallow, frog-filled bottom lands. Native Americans once canoed these waters, where now trappers bring in muskrats for their pelts and commercial fishermen bring in freshly caught carp, catfish, and snapping turtles for the discerning diner.

The Great River Road hopscotches along the rim of the rolling Mississippi, playing tag with the county and state parks along the route. Picnic areas abound for spur-of-the-moment pullovers when travelers are struck by midday hunger. The river itself offers interesting traffic: Always be prepared for a romantic steamboat—perhaps the Delta Queen or one of its sister vessels—coming round the bend upriver from New Orleans or downstream from St. Paul. At the locks and dams along the river route, stop to admire the steering proficiency of contemporary towboat captains, who muscle their cargo-laden barges into position for the next stage of their trip. The spirit of Mark Twain lives on in the state.

This is "driftless" Wisconsin, where glacial fingers of ice never reached far enough across the landscape to do the kneading and leveling work they accomplished elsewhere. As such, there are plenty of rough, scenic edges to admire, especially along the Kickapoo River Valley. Southwestern Wisconsin is one of the state's premier bird-watching locales as well, because it lies along the national flyway for migrating waterfowl—so be sure to bring binoculars, a birding book, and patience.

This is also Amish country, where boys in broad-brimmed straw hats walk alongside their dads' teams during plowing, planting, and harvesting. Wildcat Mountain State Park, near the village of Ontario and its Amish neighbors, has some of the best hiking trails in the state with its rolling hills and scenic overlooks of the horse-tilled farmlands below.

Exploration is the name of the game in this part of Wisconsin, where waterways tie their liquid threads around the towns, farms, and forests. The marvelous ribbon that is the Mississippi River entwines the heart and spirit for any traveler willing to be so captured. It is almost impossible to escape.

THE GREAT RIVER ROAD

THE ROUTE

Follow Wisconsin Highway 35 south along the Mississippi River from Alma to Prairie du Chien.

Wisconsin Highway 35, the Great River Road, provides one of Wisconsin's best scenic drives. An unparalleled vision of the Mississippi River occurs when breaking over the crest of Alma Ridge, a rocky range separating the river bottoms from Wisconsin's flatter, cow-inhabited interior. The lofty range of Belvidere Ridge is to the south, separated from the Alma bluffs by the recesses of Schultz Valley.

Most of the buildings in the town of Alma date from the late 1800s. Once they primarily served the locals, but today the refurbished structures are antique shops, trendy wine cellars, and cozy coffeehouses geared

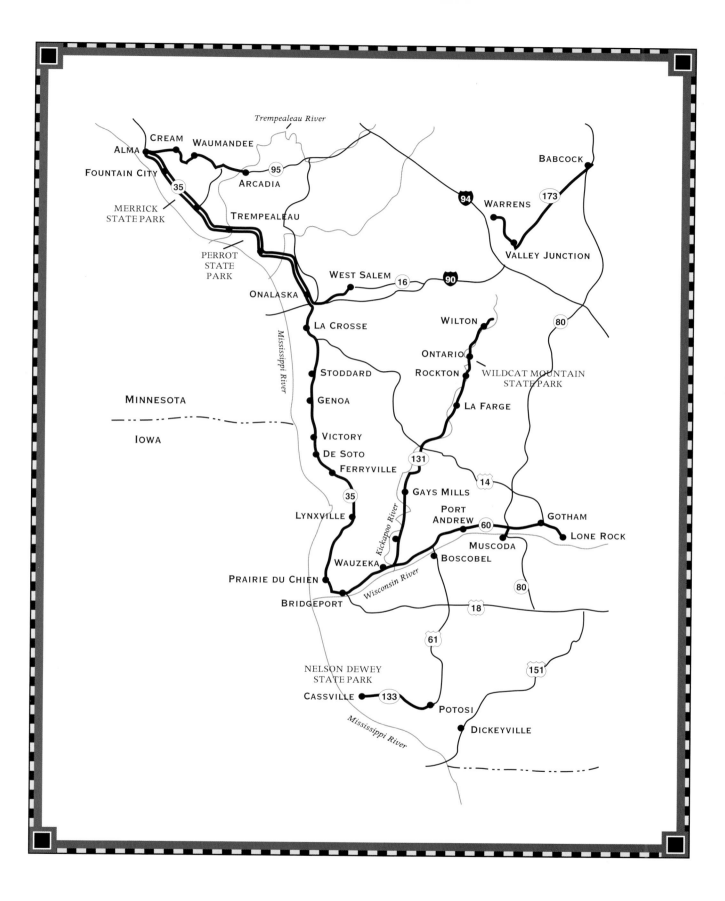

SEAN, TAMMY, AND TERRY O'ROURKE,
FROM ST. PAUL, MINNESOTA, ENJOY
THE SUNSET FROM BRADY'S BLUFF IN
PERROT STATE PARK.

RIGHT:
THE TRANQUIL WATER OF THE MISSIS-
SIPPI RIVER ROLLS SLOWLY PAST
FERRYVILLE.

ABOVE:
A BARGE GOES THROUGH LOCK AND DAM NUMBER 9 NORTH OF PRAIRIE DU CHIEN.

LEFT:
THIS PATH LEADS HIKERS TO BRADY'S BLUFF.

toward tourists. The Burlington Northern & Santa Fe Railroad (BNSF) edges along the western rim of town, the track bed only a few feet above the waterline. On the south side of Alma, just beyond the Alma Farmers Union Co-op feed and seed warehouse, are the twin stacks of the Dairyland Power Co-operative. Next comes the Great River Harbor camping site, where fat trailers line Indian Point like sunbathing terrapins.

A plant for the La Crosse Milling Company is one of the primary features of waterfront Cochrane on Highway 35 where it cuts inland about a mile. The river is separated from the roadway by a wide flood plain with a proliferation of muskrat huts. The Whitman Dam State Wildlife Area sprawls to the right on this drive south, with bald eagles, egrets, ducks, and geese making the region an ornithologist's dreamscape.

Fountain City is another community gone upscale—its craft shops explode with Amish quilting, birdhouses, and fluffy pillows. On its north side, Boone's Bike Shop has a great mural of Raggedy Ann and Andy dolls pedaling along on their cycles. Fountain City also boasts Merrick State Park, one of two excellent state parks along the section of the Great River Road between Alma and Prairie du Chien. Merrick offers year-round out-doors experiences for fishing fans, including ice angling when winter winds howl down the waterway. In milder weather, a dedicated birdwatcher can spot egrets and herons on the marshes near the park.

Lock and Dam Number 5A is two miles south of town, with the Minnesota city of Winona on the western bank of the Mississippi. One of the only stoplights encountered on this stretch of the Great River Road is at the junction of Highways 35 and 54, where 54 crosses the Mississippi. Keep driving to reach the Trempealeau National Wildlife Refuge, which features the Great River State Biking/Hiking Trail for birdwatchers and bicyclists.

Perrot State Park covers 1,243 acres tucked amid the 500-foot-high bluffs south of where the Trempealeau and Mississippi Rivers marry. The park has some of the most distinct vistas along this stretch of western Wisconsin, especially from Brady's Bluff, the Black Walnut Nature Trail, Perrot Ridge, or the Riverview Overlook.

You can't miss the town of Trempealeau, with its fluttering United States flags lining Highway 35. A parking lot for the Great River State Trail is just south of town; from there, you will continue south through Onalaska and La Crosse before hitting a more rural stretch of Highway 35 again. The high bluffline of craggy Mount La Crosse lies to the east. The Upper Mississippi Flyway—a major migratory route for birds of all feath-ers—runs here, as well. A bass-shaped mailbox near the village of Stoddard is a reminder that folks in these parts take their angling very seriously.

Farther south, at the town of Genoa, is Lock and Dam Number 8. It is located 679 miles above the mouth of the Ohio River and is one of the largest lock and dam systems on the upper Mississippi. The massive struc-ture is built in a foundation of sand and gravel across the 110-foot-wide channel. There is an 11-foot lift from the upper to the lower pool. The dam was built for $6,702,500, in a project approved by Congress in 1935. In May 1937, a battery of fifteen gates closed, flooding 18,592 acres of land. The dam was largely completed by 1938, and was one of twenty-six such units built by the government on the Mississippi to improve navigation at the time from the Twin Cities to the Missouri River.

History buffs will be interested in the town of Victory. At Battle Hollow Road—about two miles south of the village, beneath the 1,339-foot rise of Battle Bluff—a marble marker commemorates the conclusion of the Black Hawk War of 1832. Sac and Fox Indians had fled their Illinois homeland and were trying to escape across the Mississippi to Iowa, but an armed steamboat had come upriver from Fort Crawford in Prairie du Chien to block their retreat. Of the thousand or so Indians hiding in the area, 150 were immediately killed when the gunboat opened fire. Most of the survivors who made it across the rough water were massacred by Sioux enemies in an ambush on the Iowa riverbank.

South of De Soto, which lies on the Vernon and Crawford County line, is Ferryville, the self-proclaimed "Sportsman's Paradise." The town was originally called Humblebush, but when a ferry was launched to the Iowa side in the nineteenth century, residents felt a name change was appropriate.

The Great River Road passes Lynxville and Lock and Dam Number 9 and plunges next into Prairie du Chien, which is the second oldest city in Wisconsin, founded in 1781 by French Canadian trappers. It offers attractions like the Villa Louis, the former home of fur trader Hercules Dousman, who owned hundreds of acres around the first village in the mid 1800s. Today, his house sits on twenty-five acres of St. Feriole Island and is owned by the State Historical Society of Wisconsin.

THIS VINTAGE POSTCARD PROVIDES A ROMANTIC VIEW OF PRAIRIE DU CHIEN'S VILLA LOUIS.

Highway 35 continues its up-and-down land-bound trip deeper through southwestern Wisconsin, after its start at Prescott where U.S. Highway 10 crosses the St. Croix River near Hastings, Minnesota. The Great River Road then runs along the perimeter of Wisconsin and on into Illinois. Our tour of the Great River Road concludes at the Wisconsin Division of Tourism information office near Prairie du Chien on the Mississippi. A statue of explorer Jacques Marquette sits atop a high pedestal at the rear of the structure and waves from his vantage point. He and his paddling partner, Louis Jolliet, came down the Wisconsin River to where it joins the Mississippi over three hundred years ago. On June 17, 1673, Marquette, Jolliet, and their companions were the first Europeans to see this part of the Mississippi. The area of waterway visions is still a majestic sight today as the eagles soar overhead, the muskrats build their homes below, and the river just keeps chuggin' along.

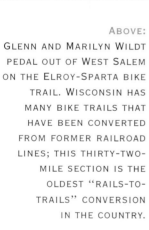

ABOVE:
GLENN AND MARILYN WILDT
PEDAL OUT OF WEST SALEM
ON THE ELROY-SPARTA BIKE
TRAIL. WISCONSIN HAS
MANY BIKE TRAILS THAT
HAVE BEEN CONVERTED
FROM FORMER RAILROAD
LINES; THIS THIRTY-TWO-
MILE SECTION IS THE
OLDEST "RAILS-TO-
TRAILS" CONVERSION
IN THE COUNTRY.

RIGHT:
A VISITOR CAN EASILY
IMAGINE HAMLIN GARLAND
WORKING IN HIS STUDY AT
THE HAMLIN GARLAND
HOUSE IN WEST SALEM.

A CORNFIELD STANDS BESIDE WISCONSIN HIGHWAY 95, WEST OF ARCADIA.

THE ROUTE

From Arcadia, take Wisconsin Highway 95 west to County Road E. Follow E west to the town of Alma. Drive south on Wisconsin Highway 35 and shoot east on Interstate 90 to pick up Wisconsin Highway 16. Drive east on 16 to the town of West Salem.

As you head west out of the village of Arcadia and drive along Wisconsin Highway 95 keep one eye peeled for the narrow, but paved, County Road E as you leave Trempealeau County. Ahead are the tree-shrouded peaks of Buffalo County. Jouncing across the Green Bay & Western railroad tracks on the far side of the town, travelers cut through an early morning mist that rests quilt-like over the fields surrounding the town.

This is coulee country of western Wisconsin, where backroads north and south of La Crosse lead deep into the region's mystical valleys. The word "coulee" is a derivative of the French *couleé*, referring to a deep ravine, usually dry in the summer but swollen with rain during the shoulder seasons of spring and autumn. Pulitzer Prize–winning author Hamlin Garland, who lived in the village of West Salem, often wrote about the farmers who struggled in this area in the tough years after the Civil War. His vivid descriptions of the Wisconsin motherland still ring true.

In the 1850s, Wisconsin formed several counties along its rugged western frontier. Among them, today's La Crosse, Monroe, Juneau, Vernon, Jackson, and Trempealeau Counties are linked in the Coulee Pathways Heritage Tourism Project, a local promotion to attract visitors.

The Trempealeau River slogs along just to the south of Highway 95, gurgling a slow, lazy way through Arcadia at the junction of the serpentine Trempealeau River and Turon Creek. It's here that you'll turn off on E, spin to the northwest, and drive through the deep shadows of Irish Valley, part of Wisconsin's lofty Montana Ridge whose top is often obscured by low-hanging clouds.

While descending into Irish Valley, the steeple of Waumandee's St. Boniface Catholic Church can be seen ahead overlooking the village. It's another three miles west, where Highway E meets with County Road U, that you enter the town of Waumandee, home of the Golden Hornets high school basketball team. Staying on E, cross Wisconsin Highway 88 and continue west, steadily rising as the valley drops away and the county road crawls higher into the hills. Silos are watchtowers, offering views of the world to pigeons perched on the ramparts.

As the car creeps higher toward the summit separating the heartland of Wisconsin from the Mississippi River, Waumandee becomes a smudge of Monopoly-sized buildings, and St. Boniface eventually disappears. Then you are over the hill and careening down the back slope to the rivertown of Alma. From there, take a ride south on Highway 35, the Great River Road, and east on Wisconsin Highway 16 to reach the village of West Salem.

In West Salem—population circa 4,000—take time to visit author Hamlin Garland's home at 357 West Garland Street, which is open from May through September. With numerous novels, dozens of short stories, and many articles to his credit, Garland won the fabled Pulitzer in 1921 for *A Daughter of the Middle Border*, one of four major autobiographical works.

Garland, the oldest of the family's four children, was born on September 14, 1860, in a cabin on the east side of town. The artifact-packed Garland homesite, now operated as a museum by the West Salem Historical Society, was purchased by the author in 1893 on behalf of his mother. Garland lived there until 1915, when he moved to California where he died in 1940. His ashes were returned to West Salem for burial in the family plot at Neshonoc Cemetery. A self-guided road tour along Rustic Road 31, indicated by the state's brown markers, takes the traveler past the Hamlin Garland Homestead. The tour—primarily made up of city streets—starts out as County Road B near the B&H Radiator Shop.

GARLAND SPINS REALISTIC FRONTIER TALES

One of Hamlin Garland's most famous collections of short stories, *Main Travelled Roads,* was first released in 1891. In his frontispiece, he described his subject:

"The main travelled road in the West (as everywhere) is hot and dusty in summer, and desolate and drear with mud in fall and spring, but is does sometimes cross a rich meadow where the songs of the larks and bobolinks and blackbirds are tangled. Follow it far enough, it may lead past a bend in the river where the water laughs eternally over its shadows.

Mainly it is long and wearyful, and has a dull little town at one end and a home of toil at the other. Like the main travelled road of life, it is traversed by many classes of people, but the poor and weary predominate."

HAMLIN GARLAND POSED FOR THIS PORTRAIT IN 1891. (WISCONSIN HISTORICAL SOCIETY, WHI (X3) 32275)

After exploring Garland's life, head south out of West Salem on County Road M for an alternate country drive. Passing the feed mill and Coulee Farm Supply, motor under Interstate 90 where the wide cornfields of Wisconsin beckon. The well-kept Nuttleman Farm straddles the roadway at the intersection of County Roads M and B. Continue south on M, then turn right on County O and proceed through the unincorporated hamlet of Barre Mills to pick up OA, a gravel county road that edges south through Garbers Coulee near the Roadside Tavern. The road proceeds past the Schombergs' spread where the thick perfume of feeding cattle rests heavily in the air. OA then crawls atop St. Joseph's Ridge—the valley floor below showing off neat farmsteads with straight green rows of corn and yellowing fields of wheat. From OA, angle to the southwest via County Road FO, leaving the gravel behind as you pick up Wisconsin Highway 33. Double back east along the high bluff to County Road YY and turn right to continue traveling southwest. Breidel Coulee falls away on both sides as the road connects with U.S. Highway 14/61. From this major roadway it is only about three miles west to Highway 35, the Great River Road.

FACING PAGE:

A CRANBERRY BOAT SITS IN A CRANBERRY BOG.

ABOVE:

IN A BOG FLOODED FOR HARVESTING, LLOYD GRIFFIN ATTACHES A ROW OF "BOATS" TO HIS CRANBERRY BEATER. GRIFFIN'S MACHINE GENTLY BEATS THE RIPE BERRIES OFF THE VINE AND INTO THE WATER SO THEY WILL NOT BE HARMED. THEY ARE THEN FUNNELED INTO THE BOATS BY ANOTHER MACHINE. GRIFFIN WORKS FOR NORTHLAND CRANBERRY INCORPORATED IN WARRENS, A SMALL TOWN THAT SWELLS WITH VISITORS EVERY SEPTEMBER DURING ITS CRANBERRY FESTIVAL.

Beginning in Babcock, drive southwest on Wisconsin Highway 173 to Valley Junction. From there, take County Roads N north and EW west to Warrens.

Wisconsin Highway 173 runs straight as the proverbial arrow from tiny Valley Junction, about three miles northeast of Interstate 94, on to Babcock where it ricochets off Wisconsin Highway 80 to the Sandhill Wildlife Area. The highway then zings almost due east to disappear into the downtown of Wisconsin Rapids, a former logging town now home to pulp mills and fruit processing plants.

Along 173's more than forty quiet miles are cranberry bogs, buffalo, and the occasional wolf. Between ninety and one hundred protected wolves live in Wisconsin. The Wildcat Mound, Bear Bluff, and South Bluff packs travel in a wide range that runs southeast to northwest in central Wisconsin, touching corners of Juneau, Wood, Monroe, Jackson, Clark, and Eau Claire Counties. Packs roam the thickets and abandoned farm fields of the Meadow Valley and Wood County state wildlife areas and the sprawling expanse of the 40,000-acre Necedah National Wildlife Refuge.

The Sandhill Wildlife Area, once the bottom of ancient Lake Wisconsin, is a sandstone plateau that was submerged by an inland sea about 500 million years ago. Originally, the land was covered with oak and white and red pine, which naturally attracted the lumbermen. The timber was clear-cut between the 1850s and 1880s, allowing farmers to claim homesteads. Floating steam dredges were used to create 750 miles of drainage ditches that spiderwebbed over what now makes up the preserve. While the peat soil was rich, it was too acidic for most crops. This—combined with raging wildfires and unexpected summer frosts—doomed agricultural pursuits. The Great Depression cleared out remaining farmers.

In the 1930s, much of this "wasteland" was purchased by Wallace Grange, who enclosed 9,460 acres with an eight-foot-high fence to create his Sandhill Game Farm. Grange was the state's first superintendent of Game Management for the Wisconsin Conservation Department—now the Department of Natural Resources—serving in that post from 1928 to 1930. Even in the small space of Sandhill, Grange did so well raising game that many of his deer were shipped around the country to help repopulate stock. He also peddled ducks to Chicago and New York restaurants and grouse to Western game farms. In 1962, Grange sold his property to the state, on the condition it be used as wildlife education center, which is accessible on Wood County Road X off Highway 80, a mile or so south of Babcock.

Today, Sandhill is one of few such multiuse sites in the country. It offers an outdoor skills center, where guests experience canoe camping, hear eerie coyote calls at night, and identify the croaks of spring frogs. Hunting clinics aid bow, gun, and even camera buffs.

Motorists can drive along the preserve's fourteen-mile Trumpeter Trail, open from April to October. There are numerous pullovers for birdwatchers, and bison can be observed along the Trumpeter as well. The fifteen or so bison that now live in a 260-acre enclosure are the descendants of a herd started by Grange in the 1940s. One tower from which to see the animals is atop the billion-year-old, 200-foot-high North Bluff, a hummock made of Precambrian quartz-like rock. The panorama from the bluff's brow shows off twenty miles of surrounding countryside. Another tower overlooks Sandhill's Gallegher Marsh with its plentiful supply of herons.

In addition to wildlife, central Wisconsin is replete with cranberry bogs. Growers utilize cultivation beds that are between two and four acres in size, where the top layer of soil has been scraped off to provide earth for dikes around each bed. New plantings are developed from vine cuttings taken from older beds and planted in the new site. During the growing season, the vines are irrigated, and weed and insect control is tightly monitored. It takes up to three years for the new vines to become established, with production not starting for at least five years.

Tour the bogs when the cranberry flowers blossom in the spring, pollinated by bees brought in by the growers. At harvest time in September, the beds are flooded. The berries used in processed foods are knocked from their vines by machines with large rotating paddles called beaters. They are then floated into one corner of the bed where they can be picked up and taken to a processing plant. Berries to be used as fresh produce are harvested by a machine with a rotating head that has retractable teeth to comb the vines and remove the fruit. In the winter, the beds are flooded, with the unfrozen water drained out from under the ice. The vines can then lie dormant under several inches of ice and air, which protects them from the tough Wisconsin chill, wind, and snow. About every four years, sand is spread across the ice. When the ice melts, the sand is subsequently added to the soil mixture to help ensure healthy new growth.

The berries grown in Wisconsin can be sweetened and dried or used for sauce, juice, candles, grilling marinades, tea, and dozens of additional products. During the annual harvest, Warrens is the state's Cranberry Capital, home to a large cranberry festival usually held on the last weekend in September. The celebration includes tours of area bogs, spaghetti feed, biggest berry competition, parade, steak fry, farmers' market, and other farm-country hoopla.

THE KICKAPOO RIVER VALLEY

Even a crow would be confused flying along the sixty-five miles of the Kickapoo River Valley. Called the "crookedest riverway in Wisconsin," the shallow river bobs, weaves, and turns like a middleweight boxer. In the Ho-Chunk dialect, *Kickapoo* means "one which goes here, then there." Aptly put.

The river promenades roughly 125 miles from the headwaters near Wilton south to Wauzeka, where it wriggles into the Wisconsin River. The Kickapoo cuts its zigzagging path through the Wisconsin limestone,

THE ROUTE

Take Wisconsin Highway 131 south from Wilton to Wisconsin Highway 60. Follow 60 west into Wauzeka.

These apple trees at Gays Mills are in full spring blossom.

BLUEBELLS BLOOM ALONG WISCONSIN HIGHWAY 131, SOUTH OF ONTARIO.

WILDCAT MOUNTAIN PARK NATURALIST BARB SCHIEFFER (AT THE STERN OF THE CANOE) PADDLES ON THE KICKAPOO RIVER WITH HER DAUGHTER LISA AND THEIR TWO DOGS.

forming a valley that ranges from a narrow gap to about a mile wide. Dozens of smaller streams, which are excellent for canoeing, feed into the major flowage.

The best route to see the river is along a seventy-mile stretch of Wisconsin Highway 131, extending from one end of the watershed to the other. In the south, broad, flat farmland spreads its rows of corn and wheat as a green-and-yellow tapestry. There are also forests of ash and oak throughout the region, with ridgelines heavy with umbrella-like maples. This corner of Wisconsin, tucked into the southwest "driftless" area, escaped the rolling and crunching of glaciers. As a result, much of the countryside here remained rugged, rather than flat. The hilly skyline is as raggedy as a broken comb.

The state government has its eye on the wriggly highway, however. The Department of Transportation's vision of widening and straightening the road over a 7.8-mile stretch between Ontario and Rockton has outdoors-lovers up in arms. They fear that the effects of the "improvements" will adversely affect the region's ecologically sensitive areas. Lawsuits demanding more environmental study on the area are causing a flurry of action over the proposal.

Tradition and preservation are important to the people of this region. The Ho-Chunk Nation and a state-approved board manage the Kickapoo Valley Reserve, an oak- and pine-covered tract between the villages of La Farge and Ontario. These 8,569-acres are set aside for outdoor recreational and environmental purposes. The reserve was originally a flood-control project proposed in the late 1960s and early 1970s that was abandoned in 1973. Today, the Kickapoo Valley Reserve has more than one hundred species of nesting fowl such as northern cardinals, rose-breasted grosbeaks, scarlet tanagers, sparrows, buntings, and a host of others. There are numerous entry points to the reserve from Highway 131, with an excellent overlook about two miles north of La Farge near Harris Road. The northern end of the reserve abuts the south side of Wildcat Mountain State Park.

Wildcat is a favorite place to hike, high as it is overlooking the valley. The hilltop on which the park sits is thick with pines, oaks, and maples and was originally a farm. Since 1948, the park has been expanded to around 3,500 acres. The main entrance, one mile south of Ontario on Wisconsin Highway 33, can be reached from Highway 131 via County Road F.

Hiking the park is a refreshing challenge, especially on Old Settler's Trail. The trailhead is an overlook with a soul-sensitizing view. A smattering of earth tones round out nature's palette here, where the scarred brown cliffsides and the rough riverbanks open to the damp sky. A section of the trail was originally used by the first settlers, where they herded their half-wild cattle out of the dense forests and onto the high pastures. Steps made from logs help in navigating some of the rougher parts of the trail, and a bench halfway along the route is situated at exactly the correct spot for tired hikers.

Mount Pisgah Hemlock Hardwoods Natural Area is just south of Wildcat near the intersection of Highway 33 and County Road F, 1,220 feet above sea level and forty-five miles north of the Kickapoo's union with the Wisconsin River. The "kuk-kuk-kuk" of huge, pileated woodpeckers echoes rhythmically through the patches of hardy basswood back a few hundred feet from the poke-along river. At the very top of the area's peak is a spectacular view that opens up the Kickapoo Valley world.

At the hub of this world is Wisconsin's apple-growing center of Gays Mills, which celebrated its sesquicentennial in 1998. Land on both sides of the Kickapoo River were excellent for planting orchards in style of the folk legend Johnny Appleseed—not that he was ever around these parts, but the early settlers of the 1800s knew what they were doing. In 1905, an apple display by area farmers took first prize at the Wisconsin State Fair and captured national honors shortly afterwards at a show in New York. Today, more than a thousand acres of fruit trees offer their spring perfume and autumn harvest, the latter always celebrated early in October with an annual apple fest that includes parades, apple pie sales, and general good fun.

THE WISCONSIN RIVER VALLEY

Even in winter, driving along the Wisconsin River is a thrill. The waterway is quiet under pillowed drifts that extend from the bluffs on the north side of Wisconsin Highway 60, across the road, into the ditch, over the marsh, and atop the river. The lights of far off small towns are faint as late afternoon droops its heavy eyelids on a cold, waning day. Warmer times of the year bring more pleasant driving along Highway 60, when the two-laner seems to rise and fall like a Wisconsin State Fair carnival ride.

Concentrate on the leg of Highway 60 west of Prairie du Sac, neighboring Sauk City, and the Lower Wisconsin River State Wildlife Area, a sprawling state-managed acreage with broad-winged hawks, wild turkeys, and yellow-billed cuckoos.

At Lone Rock, note that it is the "coldest [town] in the nation [but] with a warm heart." On January 30, 1951, at 6:00 A.M., the temperature plummeted to 53 degrees below zero in Lone Rock, putting the community on the weather map forever.

About seven miles west of Lone Rock is tiny Gotham, divided by Highway 60 and U.S. Highway 14. After Gotham, the road becomes more winding where motorists play Red Rover with the river—sometimes running closer, sometimes stepping back, but always within sight and sense of the flowage. Canoe rental outlets abound between Gotham and Muscoda, on a stretch of the river noted for its boating. This crossroads reaches across the river to Muscoda via the Wisconsin Highway 80 bridge. Muscoda is the state's morel mushroom capital, and the surrounding countryside is well known to gourmets seeking these delicious delights. "Muscoda," a

THE ROUTE

Take Wisconsin Highway 60 west from Lone Rock to the Wisconsin Highway 80 bridge. Cross the river south to Muscoda before returning to Highway 60 west to Port Andrew. Continue west until 60 intersects with U.S. Highway 61, where a bridge runs south to Boscobel. Resume driving west on 60 to Bridgeport, then follow U.S. Highway 18 west into Prairie du Chien.

LEFT:
SUMAC GROWS ON A STEEP HILLSIDE ALONG WISCONSIN
HIGHWAY 60 AS THE ROAD TWISTS AND TURNS WITH THE
WISCONSIN RIVER.

ABOVE:
MOREL MUSHROOMS GROW IN ABUNDANCE NEAR MUSCODA,
SOUTH OF WISCONSIN HIGHWAY 60. THE BEST TIME TO FIND
THEM IS USUALLY IN MAY, BUT DON'T EXPECT MUCH HELP
FROM THE LOCALS—THEY'LL GIVE YOU DIRECTIONS TO
ALMOST ANYWHERE EXCEPT THEIR SECRET MOREL PATCHES.

corruption of the native term *mash-ko-deng,* meaning "meadow," is also home to the Ho-Chunk Nation Farms, which raises vegetables for sale. In addition to their farming, the Ho-Chunk—formerly known as the Winnebago—operate a large casino in the Wisconsin Dells.

One of the major towns in the area is Boscobel. *Bosque belle,* or "beautiful woods," was discovered by explorers Jacques Marquette and Louis Jolliet in 1673 on their journey toward the Mississippi River. Today, the town is known both as the Wild Turkey Capital of Wisconsin and the home of the Gideon Bible, which is found in hotel nightstand drawers around the world. The Boscobel Hotel, now listed on the National Register of Historic Places, was built in 1865. It was 1898, when the hotel was known as the Central House, that two traveling salesmen came up with the idea of placing bibles in hostelry rooms. The famous structure is now managed by the Boscobel Area Heritage Museum. The town is also home of the last remaining Grand Army of the Republic meeting hall in Wisconsin, and the Boscobel Cemetery is the final resting place of 178 Civil War veterans. Military buffs from around the Midwest flock to Boscobel on the first weekend of each August for a large battlefield reenactment.

Highway 60 becomes Mill Street when it reaches Boydtown, which consists of three houses, a barn, and a silo. As 60 continues, the lofty bump of Harris Ridge rears to the right and several small sandbars can be spotted in the river to the left. Canoeists often beach on these hummocks for a bit of extra sunbathing. Little Kickapoo Creek, just west of Wauzeka, plunges down the rock slopes of Dutch Ridge to cross under Highway 60 and flow into the Wisconsin River. It is one of a number of small parallel waterways, including Bush and Gran Grae Creeks, which also flow out of the adjoining hills. The Rhein and Tucker Hollows and the Vineyard Coulee—consecutive sharp-edged slopes that rear skyward through thick stands of oak—further distinguish the landscape.

Highway 60 passes Bridgeport before morphing into U.S. Highway 18 and Wisconsin Highway 35 and rushing down a hill into Prairie du Chien. The first American flag flown over Wisconsin territory fluttered in a September breeze near Prairie du Chien when Lieutenant Zebulon Pike explored the vicinity in 1805. He was a latecomer to town, however, compared to the centuries of Native Americans who called this area home and the decades of French-Canadian voyageurs who settled down here after they retired from the fur trade.

Whether driving through snow or summer sun, Highway 60 presents a glorious panorama of Wisconsin. The drive offers history, fabulous flora and fauna, and an all-around feeling of escape that can be taken in small enough chunks to allow plenty of time to savor each section of the trip.

GLORIOUS GRANT COUNTY

The late afternoon sun splashes honey-hued rays over the oaks that blanket Grant County's granite hills. Cicadas hum amid the purple coneflowers, yellow daisies, and goldenrod carpeting the ditches along Wisconsin Highway 133, the main—but narrow—artery connecting inland Potosi and Cassville on the rolling Mississippi.

Grant County is one of the leading agricultural regions of the Midwest, ranking among the top counties in Wisconsin for production of beef cattle, hogs, oats, and alfalfa, and third in the state for its number of dairy cows. In the good old days, however, lead was the product of choice.

French explorer Nicholas Perrot began mining valuable lead and onyx in southwestern Wisconsin during the late seventeenth century, but it wasn't until 1827, with the signing of the Winnebago Peace Treaty, that newcomers arrived in force to quarry the region in earnest. Armed with shovels and picks, settlers began digging lead from Lancaster to Platteville to New Diggings to Shullsburg to Mineral Point. Their long-abandoned pits—now shallow, grass- and tree-covered depressions in the ground—can still be seen while driving the county sideroads. British Hollow, Happy Hollow, and Dutch Hollow Roads east of Potosi are among the best routes for pit sightings. Each is readily accessible from Highway 133.

Some miners lived in caves dug into the sides of the ridge walls, which were reminiscent of dank badger burrows. Thus was born Wisconsin's nickname as the "Badger State." A collection of patched canvas tents, rude huts, and ramshackle storefronts near the "burrows" eventually evolved into the village of Snake Hollow, later renamed Potosi. The community became the leading river port in the upper Midwest in the 1820s and 1830s as tons of lead flowed from its hills down the Mississippi to New Orleans or back overland to the East. St. John's Mine was one of the area's richest caches. Located along Highway 133 at the east end of Potosi, the cavern is now open for tourists.

The highway sweeps down into Potosi, making several doglegs as it continues through town as Main Street, past Gibby's Bar and the local feed store. The Ripley's Believe It Or Not cartoon strip once called this almost three-mile stretch of concrete, the "longest main street in America." Potosi and neighboring Tennyson now jointly claim the "Catfish Capital of Wisconsin" title and host an annual Catfish Festival the second week of August.

A side trip, only eight or so miles southeast of Potosi-Tennyson at the junction of Wisconsin Highway 35 and U.S. Highways 61 and 151, will take you to the Grant County village of Dickeyville. The Dickeyville Grotto is one of Wisconsin's notably quirky landmarks. The jumble of rock and

THE ROUTE

Take Wisconsin Highway 133 west from Potosi to Cassville.

CASSVILLE LEAD MINERS TAKE A BREAK IN THIS PHOTOGRAPH, CIRCA 1900. (WISCONSIN HISTORICAL SOCIETY, WHI (F4) 304)

ABOVE:
THE ANNUAL FIREMEN'S CATFISH
FESTIVAL IN POTOSI STARTS WITH A
PARADE.

RIGHT:
CATFISH PRINCESSES NICOLE AMES,
ARIEL STEINER, ALYSSA REUTER, KATIE
REYNOLDS, AND HANNAH SCHOLBROCK
WAIT FOR THE CATFISH FESTIVAL
PARADE AND THE CHANCE TO SEE WHO
WILL BE CROWNED LITTLE MISS
CATFISH. THE WINNER IS CHOSEN BY
DRAWING A NAME FROM A HAT.

A SHRINE TO "CHRISTOPHER COLUMBUS, DISCOVERER OF AMERICA," STANDS AT THE DICKEYVILLE GROTTO.

granite handmade formations adjacent to Holy Ghost Church were erected by Father Matthias Wernerus, pastor of the parish from 1913 to 1931. Between 1925 and 1930, he constructed the mortar and concrete structures, adding gems, fancy beads, rock crystals, amber glass, coal, coral, and even knobs from old auto gearshifts to his fanciful imagery.

Wernerus built several shrines in his grotto to honor the Blessed Virgin and other religious figures, the Stations of the Cross, which depict Christ's journey from his trial to crucifixion, and several patriotic pieces. Flowers around the grotto add explosions of fragrance and color.

West of Potosi, Highway 133 continues nineteen miles toward Cassville. The Cassville Car Ferry, which crosses the Mississippi River, docks at Wall Street, about two blocks west of Highway 133, Cassville's main street. The ferry links with Turkey River, Iowa, and Iowa Highway 52/C9Y near Millville. In the 1920s, folks used to call the over-and-back ferry ride "Looping the Loop." Piling kids, dogs, grandparents, and picnic baskets into their flivvers, they took the car ferry over the river from Cassville and drove north thirty miles to McGregor, Iowa, where they crossed the bridge back into Wisconsin at Prairie du Chien. From there, they would return a serpentine way home on Grant County Roads C to X to VV. A different route took them from the ferry crossing south thirty miles to Dubuque, Iowa, where they would cross into Illinois, driving back to Cassville via Highways 35 and 133.

The town's quiet way of life attracted ex-governor Nelson Dewey, who built a mansion on the bluffs above the river. His home is now part of the Nelson Dewey State Park, located across the highway from Stonefield

CASSVILLE WAS ONCE IN THE RUNNING TO BE THE CAPITAL OF THE WISCONSIN TERRITORY. THE RED BRICK BUILDING ON THE LEFT IN THIS PHOTO WAS BUILT TO HOUSE THE NEW GOVERNMENT, BUT WHEN BELMONT WAS CHOSEN AS THE FIRST TERRITORIAL CAPITAL, THE BUILDING BECAME A HOTEL. IT IS NOW CALLED THE DENNISTON HOUSE, AND CASSVILLE—BYPASSED BY THE GOVERNMENT—HAS REMAINED A SMALL, SLEEPY TOWN ALONG THE MISSISSIPPI RIVER.

DEWEY EARNS FIRST STATE GOVERNORSHIP

Nelson Dewey was Wisconsin's first state governor. The popular political leader was not a Wisconsinite by birth, however. He was born on December 19, 1813, in Lebanon, Connecticut, and grew up in New York State. The lure of the West and its promise of adventure took Dewey away from his East Coast life. When he settled in the rough-and-ready mining town of Lancaster, Wisconsin, he saw the need for an aggressive lawyer. Dewey subsequently studied law and quickly became active in politics. He served as Grant County's first registrar of deeds from 1836 to 1842 and moved on to the territorial legislative assembly in 1838. The silver-tongued young man was quickly named as the assembly's speaker and was selected as its president during the 1842–1846 session. Dewey kept climbing up the political ladder and became the state's governor in 1848. During his first term, he married Kate Dunn,

GOVERNOR NELSON DEWEY LOOKS STERN IN THIS IMPRESSIVE PORTRAIT. (WISCONSIN HISTORICAL SOCIETY, WHI (X3) 1454)

the lively daughter of Charles Dunn, the former territorial chief justice. Dewey was reelected for a second term in 1850.

Using his contacts in the political and business world, Dewey's entrepreneurial spirit followed all sorts of economic opportunities, which included managing a large, successful farming operation and helping develop the lead mines along the Mississippi River near his new house. Dewey finally retired from politics to run his farm, yet he kept up his varied interests and remained an active member of the Democratic Party. He regularly attended its state conventions and was a presidential elector in 1888.

Dewey was interested in many social causes and was also an avid historian, as is proved by his election to president of the Wisconsin Historical Society in 1849. Dewey died on July 21, 1889, and is buried in Lancaster.

Village and State Farm Museum. The "village" is a replica of an 1890s small town and features a blacksmith shop, stores, a church, and other buildings typical of the era.

A great summer place to camp in Wisconsin is at one of the primitive sites atop the ridgeline of Nelson Dewey Park, overlooking the Mississippi. The park's 250 acres were once part of the former governor's 2,000-acre estate. After his death in 1889, the land and Dewey's home went through a parade of owners before several local governmental groups purchased 720 acres and the house in 1936. The park is on Grant County Road VV, about two miles north of Cassville.

An all-inclusive hike through the park skirts the bluffs, wends through thick oak woods, and edges past thousand-year-old effigy mounds. The Dewey Heights portion of the trail is especially breathtaking, with several hundred feet of air between the hiker and the valley floor. As the soft summer day edges into night, the Midas glow of the full moon spills its gold down along the Mississippi. This is Grant County at its best.

PART IV

SOUTH CENTRAL:
THE HEART OF WISCONSIN

FACING PAGE:

A SHORT, WELL-MARKED TRAIL LEADS TO STEPHENS' FALLS IN GOVERNOR DODGE STATE PARK, SOUTH OF SPRING GREEN. THE PARK HAS OVER 5,000 ACRES OF LAND AND TWO LAKES.

ABOVE:

TREES CLIMB A BLUFF ON THE SOUTH SHORE OF DEVIL'S LAKE.

Seen from overhead, the Wisconsin River has more curves than a high school geometry lesson. It loops and winds for 430 miles from its birthplace at the boundary between Wisconsin and the Upper Peninsula of Michigan to its junction with the Mississippi River at Prairie du Chien. With its numerous tributaries, the flowage drains more than twelve thousand square miles of central Wisconsin.

Crossing the Wisconsin River between April and December on the *Colsac II* ferryboat at the town of Merrimac is a good adventure. The ford here has been utilized since the 1840s, and the free trip across takes only about ten minutes. In early July, the boat provides one of the best photographic vantage points from which to view the Great Circus Parade train as it rumbles south from the Circus World Museum in nearby Baraboo, the former winter quarters of the old Ringling Brothers Circus, to Milwaukee. The train, laden with exquisitely refurbished old-time circus wagons, crosses a railroad bridge near the ferry crossing. The wagons are then showcased on Milwaukee's Lake Michigan waterfront for several days prior to a gigantic, colossal, stupendous "hold-yer-hosses-here-come-the-elephants" procession through downtown.

South Central Wisconsin is also Frank Lloyd Wright country. The renowned architect honed his prairie-style design techniques at Taliesin, Wright's home and studio, which overlooks the Wisconsin River's willow-shaded bends and sandbars near Spring Green.

Farther south—toward the Illinois border—the inquisitive traveler can meander along rustic roads throughout the crop-rich farmlands, where corn is higher than an elephant's eye early in the season. Early Swiss émigrés were reminded of the rolling hills of home when they arrived near what is now New Glarus to establish prosperous dairy operations.

Down here, when someone says, "Cheese," they mean really, really good cheese. Because of the lush grass, pampered Holsteins and Guernseys in these parts seem to smile, a factor that naturally aids in the production of the world's best dairy products. Numerous cheese plants throughout the area open their doors for tours and plenty of sampling. The best time to arrive is early in the morning, when most of the operations are underway. And remember: You have not experienced Wisconsin until you purchase a bag of the delightfully squeaky munchables called cheese curds.

LEVEE ROAD

THE ROUTE

From Portage, follow Rustic Road 49 (Levee Road) west to its intersection with County Road T, just north of Interstate 94.

The mist, with its embrace of shredded gauze, rises heavily over the backwaters of the turgid Wisconsin River near Portage. The summer sun has not yet yawned awake enough to dispel the moist dawn air. A gargantuan carp rolls slowly to the surface of the river, insolently flipping its tail and then disappearing. From the opposite bank to the north, a muskrat splashes and a great blue heron sweeps along the tree-shrouded shoreline. Puddles along Levee Road, on the southern edge of a dike keeping the river water

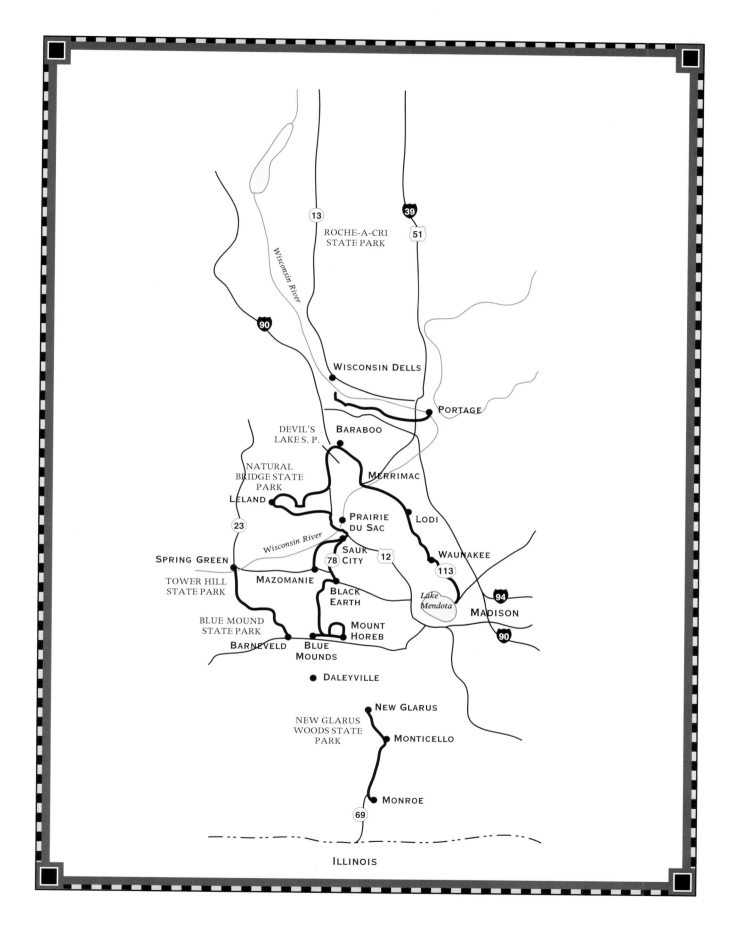

DAWN BREAKS ON THE WISCONSIN RIVER WITH A NEARLY FULL MOON OVER LEVEE ROAD.

TALL GRASS GROWS HIGH AND WILD ALONG LEVEE ROAD.

NINA LEOPOLD BRADLEY, DAUGHTER OF WISCONSIN'S FAMOUS NATURALIST ALDO LEOPOLD, AND HER HUSBAND, CHARLES, STAND IN THE INDIAN GRASS THAT THEY PLANTED BY HAND NEAR THEIR HOME ON LEVEE ROAD. THE BRADLEYS HAVE BEEN RESTORING THE PRAIRIE ON ABOUT TWENTY-FIVE ACRES OF THE LEOPOLD MEMORIAL RESERVE FOR TWO DECADES. ALTHOUGH THE LAND IS PRIVATE, AND MOTORISTS ARE ASKED TO RESPECT THAT PRIVACY, THE FRUITS OF THE BRADLEY'S LABOR ARE EVIDENT WHEN VIEWED WHILE DRIVING ALONG LEVEE ROAD.

at bay, testify to the ferocity of a late night downpour. Leaves of the rain-dampened weeping willows droop as the water drips from their slender surface.

If anyone could appreciate this scene, it would be Wisconsin's environmental guru, Aldo Leopold. Although he was not a native of Portage, the founder of the Wilderness Society maintained a summer home west of town in the 1930s and 1940s. Leopold was a noted scientist, teacher, and widely read writer. His book, *A Sand County Almanac*, is often considered among the twentieth century's best writings about conservation. In 1924, he became associate director of the U.S. Forest Products Laboratory in Madison, and in 1928 started teaching at the University of Wisconsin where he became the director of the university's Department of Game Management.

Land along this stretch of Levee Road edges through the heart of the Leopold Memorial Reserve, named for the famed naturalist. Dedicated birdwatchers can spot grasshopper sparrows, nighthawks, blackbirds, and dozens of other species.

Levee Road was officially designated as Wisconsin Rustic Road 49 in 1987, in memory of the centennial anniversary of Leopold's birth. The vista ranges from cropland to river bottom, from thick stands of oak to raspberry patches. It begins on the western edge of the city of Portage, along Fairfield Street near the intersection of Wisconsin Highway 33, and continues west to Sauk County Road T, along Interstate 94.

The city of Portage has a distinguished place in Wisconsin history. In 1673, French explorers Jacques Marquette and Louis Jolliet were the first Europeans to make their way down the Fox and Wisconsin Rivers from the French outpost in Green Bay. After traversing the mile-long portage where the city now is situated, they continued on their way downstream to meet the Mississippi River.

To safeguard the flood of new settlers as America's frontier expanded to Wisconsin, Fort Winnebago was built in the late 1820s. Indian agent John Kinzie and his wife, Juliette, were assigned here in 1830 and lived in a log building near the fort. Their rustic home and the fort's Surgeon's Quarters are state historical sites open for touring.

Portage was also home to Zona Gale, winner of the Pulitzer Prize in 1921 for the dramatization of her novel, *Miss Lulu Bett*. Not only a writer, Gale served on the University of Wisconsin board of regents from 1923 to 1929 and the Wisconsin Free Library Commission from 1923 to 1938. In 1906, after the publication of a successful first book, Gale built a home for her

ZONA GALE IS PICTURED HERE AT AGE TWENTY-TWO ALONG WITH A VINTAGE POSTCARD OF HER HOME IN PORTAGE. (WISCONSIN HISTORICAL SOCIETY, WHI (X3) 53839)

BIRTH OF THE PORTAGE CANAL

Portage businessmen needed an easy way to ship their goods between the Fox and Wisconsin Rivers, thus the Portage Canal was completed in 1849 and was expanded several times over the years to make a waterway that was two and a half miles long, seventy-five feet wide, and seven feet deep. Two locks aided navigation. Part of the massive lock gate at the Wisconsin River connection can still be seen where the old canal cuts through the heart of Portage.

A BOAT MAKES ITS WAY DOWN THE PORTAGE CANAL IN THIS PHOTOGRAPH FROM THE EARLY 1900S. (WISCONSIN HISTORICAL SOCIETY, WHI (X3) 39822)

For thirty years, lead from Prairie du Chien was carried north, lumber from northern Wisconsin forests flowed south, and farm produce traveled both directions on the canal. As roads and railroads became more cost efficient than the waterway, it became solely used for pleasure craft and finally closed in 1951. Today's canal is a remnant of its former self, with much of its flowage now routed through massive drainage pipes.

parents in Portage at 506 West Edgewater Street. The twin columns of the white Greek Revival home still earmark the building as a classy residence. It is now owned by the Women's Civic League, a social service organization founded by Gale.

Once leaving Portage, Levee Road wends its way between a dike along the river and the farmland and nature preserve. Parking is available along the way, and one suggested stop is the Pine Island State Wildlife Area about midpoint along the drive. Rolling hills lie in the southern distance, marking the far edge of the area's marshland. In 1971, Pine Island was dedicated to Ross Bennett, a Portage-area lawyer, businessman, and pioneer conservationist.

Melting glaciers after the last Ice Age created the depression that forms this area, once rich in game for Native American hunters. Early settlers used it for pastureland and haying when the boggy land dried over the summer. More extensive farming efforts failed, and interest in retaining the land as a recreation site arose as early as the 1930s. In 1952, local sport clubs and conservationists met with the state to create the wildlife area. Over the past fifty years, the project has grown to encompass most of the Wisconsin River flood plain and nearby oak uplands. Funds for the project come from hunting licenses and the state's Outdoor Recreation Action Program, as well as the federal Pittman-Robertson Act. The reedy marsh is alive with sedge, boxwood, and willow, and about 1,400 acres are planted with upland grasses, home to pheasants, deer, and wild turkeys.

The Natural Bridge is a sandstone arch that stretches over a cave, which is thought to have been used as a shelter 11,000 years ago.

In Natural Bridge State Park, the trails are often colorful.

Just beyond Pine Island is an expansive dog-training site, located along a narrow, tree-lined dirt access road about one-half mile into the woods on the south side of Levee Road. A boat landing is just to the west of the dog trial area, on the river side of the roadway. About 1,100 acres around the boat landing are set aside as a wildlife refuge during the waterfowl-hunting season, which means no entry in late autumn.

As Levee Road proceeds west, it cuts through pine plantings that stand in straight, long rows. Several public hunting grounds are along the way, and toward the far western end of the road, farmhouses and other buildings again make their appearance. It is there that Levee Road meets County Road T, and the lucky backroads traveler is greeted by an explosion of summer sun that carpets the Wisconsin cornfields.

Sauk County Adventures

The route

Beginning in Sauk City, take U.S. Highway 12 north to County Road PF, and PF west to County Road C. Turn north on C, which curves to meander east to Wisconsin Highway 12. Follow 12 north to Baraboo. From there, drive south on Wisconsin Highway 113 to Merrimac and on to Madison.

A drive north of the Wisconsin River delves deep into a land untouched by the last great crunch of glaciers. Here can be found secret backroads and hideaway highways—but, depending on the season and the weather conditions, expect to encounter bicyclists and slow-moving farm vehicles along these routes. Cross the Wisconsin River on the U.S. Highway 12 bridge at Sauk City, home of August Derleth. He was one of the state's most prolific authors, a chronicler of small-town life who churned out hundreds of articles and dozens of novels from the 1930s through the 1950s. Continue north on 12 past Tesch's Flowerland, the Dairy Systems plant, and other Sauk City businesses to County Road PF, about a mile out from the north side of town.

Turn left on PF and head west through the corn and soybean fields. The misty ridges of the Baraboo Range, a low line of eroded mountains, sleep off to the north. There's a cyclist's rest at the tree-shaded Honey Creek United Methodist Church on Church Road. The pit stop is welcome, and the flat landscape is great for leisurely biking.

Follow PF until it comes to County Road C and then turn right (north) at tiny Leland. The county road makes up the town's block-long main street. Proceed past the Honey Creek Rod and Gun Club and the Leland Millpond, where migrating mallards can be seen in spring and autumn.

About a mile and a half north of Leland on County C is Natural Bridge State Park, a 530-acre reserve with a sandstone arch that offers an opening twenty-five feet high and thirty-five feet wide. This "natural bridge" was created by wind and water erosion over tens of thousands of years. Below the rock formation is an overhang where archaeologists say humans lived almost 12,000 years ago, making it one of the earliest inhabited sites in the Midwest. To protect the site, the park was created in 1973.

After trekking through this part of Wisconsin's history, turn left on County C from the park entrance and continue to drive north to where the road rounds a bend a short quarter-mile away to hook up with Orchard

Drive. If you choose, divert from C onto Orchard Drive. It is part of Wisconsin Rustic Road 21, which leads to oak-lined Schara Road. On Orchard, you'll pass a dilapidated pioneer homestead on the left after a mile or so, with a weather-beaten log house that leans unsteadily to one side. Otherwise, continue on County C through the village of Denzer and on to U.S. Highway 12, which runs north to Baraboo.

Baraboo, the nineteenth-century winter quarters of the old Ringling Brothers Circus, is home to the Circus World Museum. Managed by the State Historical Society of Wisconsin since it opened in 1959, the museum is housed in eight of the barns and outbuildings first used by the circus as a layover between show seasons. The fifty-acre facility collects, preserves, and interprets all levels of circus history with its extensive exhibits, wagon restorations, huge research library, and summertime razzle-dazzle circus performances.

Drive south along Wisconsin Highway 113 from its origins in Baraboo to admire the prosperous farms where corn, soybeans, and hay mix their explosive palettes. Three miles south of Baraboo, Devil's Lake lies in an opening in the bluffs that rear up 500 feet above the surrounding prairie. The ancient hills were formed from sediment left behind by a shallow sea that covered this region at least a billion years ago. Over the ensuing eons, the ground buckled and rumbled as the earth matured. Glaciers then flatted much of the area, plugging one end of a valley between the bluffs and

REFURBISHED CIRCUS WAGONS RIDE ON A RAIL CAR, EN ROUTE FROM BARABOO TO MILWAUKEE.

creating the lake from its melt off, rerouting the Wisconsin River. Today's spring-fed lake varies in depth from to forty to fifty feet and covers 368 acres.

Since it is often colder closer to the lake than on the bluffs, there is an interesting mix of vegetation in this area. Sugar maples and yellow birches prefer the cooler air near the water, while the mountain maple and red elder bask in the warmer climate on the hills. This diversity creates a varied habitat for many animal species, including about 105 species of birds, forty kinds of mammals, several types of turtles, and even timber rattlesnakes.

Devil's Lake State Park encompasses 8,500 acres, with Highway 113 running along the eastern border of the grounds to provide easy access to some of the park's excellent hiking paths. Poke around Parfrey's Glen, a quarter-mile rocky gorge on the south flank of the hills around Devil's Lake. The glen is a special place for studying moss and ferns. The cold air that settles at the bottom of the bluffs creates a different habitat than that of the open, sunny air. Clintonia and mountain club moss are discovered

PARFREY'S GLEN, EAST OF DEVIL'S LAKE, IS A DELIGHTFUL PLACE FOR A WALK.

MIGRATING GEESE
FLY OVER GOOSE
POND SANCTUARY
EAST OF LODI.

THE MERRIMAC FERRY AWAITS ITS PASSENGERS.

along the small creek that tumbles down the cliffside at the far end of the glen. Bird life includes the Canada warbler and winter wren.

The glen is four miles from Devil's Lake. The most scenic route from Highway 113 is east along Solum Lane, continuing about a quarter mile to Kentview Road where you turn south on Devil's Delight Road. There are some neat twists and curves in that mile-long stretch of tree-shaded roadway. Devil's Delight links with County Road DL. Turn east again on DL and go about a mile to the parking lot at the glen entrance. For a quicker route to Parfrey's Glen, simply take DL east from 113.

Twelve miles down the Highway 113 is tree-shaded Merrimac. Pause here on pleasant days while waiting for the Merrimac Ferry to cross the Wisconsin River. A ferry landing has been located here since 1844; in 1933 the Wisconsin Department of Transportation acquired control of passage over the river. The crossing saves motorists a nine-mile drive southwest to the bridge at Prairie du Sac or a twelve-mile drive northeast to catch the Interstate 94 river passageway. The free ferry, the *Colsac II,* operates twenty-four hours a day—generally between April 15 and mid to late December. The craft is named for Columbia County on the south bank and Sauk County on the north. On bright, sunny days, the run across the water takes about ten minutes and barely a minute or so longer if the river is choppy. The *Colsac II* makes around 40,000 trips back and forth a year, carrying upwards of 195,000 vehicles annually. An underwater cable linked to the eighty-five-ton vessel's diesel engine does the actual "towing."

After crossing the river, Highway 113 takes a twisting twenty-five-mile-long route southeast toward Madison, coming into the Wisconsin capital via a bridge across an inlet of Lake Mendota.

THE LOWER WISCONSIN STATE RIVERWAY

THE ROUTE

Beginning in Black Earth, drive north on Wisconsin Highway 78 to County Road Y. Follow Y west; it will then curve south and run into the town of Mazomanie.

When the Wisconsin River sleeps, the current merely plods along, but after heavy rains, the swollen waterway roars, stirring the sand bars into a froth and shaking low-hanging willow branches. The river level can rise two to three feet within a few hours. Bald eagles and turkey vultures observe the water below from a safe distance on most breezy, sun-dappled mornings. In the backwaters, spindly legged herons cautiously splat their way across the frog-filled shallows.

The Wisconsin River begins in the Lac Vieux Desert of Vilas County on the boundary between Wisconsin and Michigan. Coursing 430 miles, the river drains 7,859,200 acres of Wisconsin, amounting to one-third of the state. The farthest downstream dam on the river is at Prairie du Sac, resulting in 92.3 miles of unimpeded flowage—the longest such stretch of waterway anywhere in the Midwest—before it empties into the Mississippi River at Prairie du Chien. This is the Lower Wisconsin State Riverway, the only project of its kind managed by the state's Department of Natural Resources. Its diverse flora and fauna, archaeology, and history make it popular with the outdoors lovers among the four million people who live within a four-hour drive of the region.

A quick route to the riverway runs northwest along Wisconsin Highway 12 from Madison. But there are more relaxed ways to reach it, if you have the time. One good backcountry drive runs from Black Earth to Sauk City. Pick up Wisconsin Highway 78, Black Earth's main street, and follow it to where it links with U.S. Highway 14. A mile and a half west of downtown Black Earth, the comfortably paved highway splits from 14, angles to the north, and loops gracefully through the countryside.

Just beyond Carter Road, which cuts to the right off of Highway 78, you'll spy a white cross on the bluff top directly ahead. The marker indicates the hilltop location of the Cedar Hills Campground, reached via Dunlop Hollow Road, which spins from 78 to the east. The road parallels shallow Dunlop Creek as it flows through the pastureland at the foot of the 900-foot-high bluff. Drive up the rough dirt road that campground owner Carl Goodwiller graded to reach the peak. Once there, a swing overlooks the valley from the vantage point of a rocky ledge.

Return to Highway 78, turn right, and again drive north. After the road bends around the bluff, you'll pass a parking lot on the right side. It's a safe spot where hikers leave their vehicles to climb to another section of the bluff. This publicly owned land is part of the Black Hawk Unit of the Lower Wisconsin State Riverway. The state purchased several hundred acres around the area in 1990 and retained some buildings from a defunct resort to be used as warming sheds for cross-country skiers and rest areas for hikers and horseback riders.

Park at the pullover about a half-mile north of the first lot. A path here edges up a sharp slope to plunge into an oak savanna. Watch out for the abundant, scratchy wild raspberry bushes. The fresh earth perfumes the air with its potpourri of wild flowers, berries, and crushed leaves.

THIS PORTRAIT OF CHIEF BLACK HAWK WAS PAINTED IN 1833. (WISCONSIN HISTORICAL SOCIETY, WHI (X3) 27087)

The ridge here, Wisconsin Heights, tells a poignant story. The hilltop was the scene of a fierce battle on July 21, 1832, when troops caught up with Sac war chief Black Hawk. He was fighting to cover the escape of his people, who were seeking a safe place to cross the Wisconsin River. The starving Native Americans had fled Illinois and were making their way through southern Wisconsin, attempting to reach Iowa on the opposite side of the Mississippi River, about sixty miles farther west. There, they hoped to find a refuge far from whites. As they made their way into Wisconsin, they were pursued by almost five thousand militia and army troops. History books call this conflict the Black Hawk War.

For a time, Racek Road shoots straight ahead.

Few things are more peaceful than watching a sunrise along Spring Valley Road near Black Earth.

On their way to Iowa, the Sac had to maneuver across Wisconsin, naturally frightening settlers along the way. Eventually, they made it to Wisconsin Heights. As the majority of Native Americans sought to cross the river, the military attempted to take the bluff. However, they were ambushed by Sac warriors hidden among the trees on the higher ground. These stalling tactics gave the bulk of Black Hawk's people the chance to make it to relative safety on the other side of the Wisconsin River. When the soldiers readied their attack the next morning, they found the entire band had slipped away—struggling all the way to the Mississippi where the army ultimately caught and massacred most of them. Eventually, the state hopes to install historical markers on the bluff describing various stages of the Battle of Wisconsin Heights. But for now, only the caw of crows in a clump of birch and ironwood calls attention to this history.

After leaving the battlefield, continue north on Highway 78 for about two miles and turn left (west) on County Road Y, which ambles along the river. You will pass the Sauk Prairie Bow Hunters–Boy Scout preserve, followed within a mile by the Wisconsin River Sportsmens Club. If you want to pause for a lazy day on the water, Blackhawk Ron's canoe rental on County Y is adjacent to the sportsmen's club. Continue slowly on Y, which passes through the Mazomanie Unit of the riverway, a perfect place for seeking the thirty-five species of warblers that live in these woodlands.

Proceeding south on Y will lead you to Mazomanie. The town name is loosely translated from Native America languages to "Iron Horse" or "Iron That Walks," referring to the early railroads.

For an interesting diversion, turn east (left) on Racek Road before reaching Mazomanie. This two-mile section of breeze-blown roadway moves directly across flat farm fields, which makes it easy to spot the white cross at Cedar Hills Campground high on the bluffs ahead. The fields on both sides of Racek Road are prime viewing areas for pheasants, the occasional wild turkey, blue-winged teals, quails, and bobolinks. After passing a small woodlot on the left and more fields, Racek Road eventually connects with Highway 78.

MOUNT HOREB AND BLUE MOUNDS

THE ROUTE

Take County Road ID west from Mount Horeb. At County Road JG, turn north and follow the road as it loops back to Mount Horeb. Resume your route west on ID to County Road F. Travel north on F until it meets with County Road KP, which will take you south into Black Earth.

Spring comes quickly to the ridges and valleys of Mount Horeb and Blue Mounds in the heart of South Central Wisconsin. Melting snowdrifts are chased away by crocuses and jack-in-the-pulpits in the ditches and along the fence rows.

Mount Horeb retains its Scandinavian heritage and hosts a Norwegian-American Fest each August. The town is also home to the nation's only Mustard Museum, housing more than four thousand specimens. It takes only ten minutes to drive through town unless pausing at Schuberts Cafe & Bakery for *lefse*, a thinly rolled potato-based confection sprinkled with powdered sugar.

Dane County Road ID rolls westward out of Mount Horeb past the trim white fences of Maple Shade Farm on the right side of the roadway and the graveled surface of the Military Ridge bike trail on the left. The thirty-nine-mile Military Ridge State Park Trail was opened in 1985 along an abandoned Chicago and Northwestern railroad line between Verona and Dodgeville. The trail runs along the top of Military Ridge, with the Wisconsin River watershed to the north and the Pecatonica and Rock Rivers flowages to the south. In the winter, cross-country skiers and snowmobilers may use the pathway.

Farther down County ID it's open fields, soft and spongy from spring rains that banished the winter's remnants. Turn north on County JG, three miles west of Mount Horeb, and aim toward Little Norway. A wooden gate on the road blocks entry to the old Norwegian farm site, which was settled in 1856 and is now open daily from May to October. The collection of buildings here includes a replica of a twelfth-century *stavekirke*. This intricate wooden church was constructed for the Colombian Exposition at the 1893 World's Fair in Chicago.

Swooping down deeper into the valley, JG curves to the right as County Road J spins off to the north at the juncture of Bohn, Elvers, and Moen Creeks. Keep following JG as it begins an easy loop back to the south. At the foot of the valley, along Moen Creek, is the Moen Creek Cottage Farm. The main cluster of white and red buildings is on the right side of JG, while chicken coops and implement sheds are on the left. One ancient log barn, resting its rump against a craggy bluffside and leaning precariously in several directions at once, is more than one hundred years old. Mark Kessenich and his wife, Linda Derrickson, raise Highland cattle and Jacob's sheep, as well as vegetables, on the ninety-some acres of meadow, tilled fields, and upland pasture that make up the farm. They are active members of Seed Savers, a national organization that cultivates old-time plants to protect species diversity by keeping a strong seed pool flourishing.

Follow County JG up a slight rise and then down again into another valley where several sharp S-curves demand careful attention. Within a mile and a half on the left is Stewart Park, one of Dane County's oldest parks. There are picnic tables, a shelter, a playground, and a small lake to explore just before reaching the north side of Mount Horeb. The trip along County JG covers approximately six meandering miles. To add on to a day's jaunt, simply return through town on the main street (County ID) and drive west again. Instead of turning north on JG as you previously did, continue along ID to County Road F. There you'll find a well-marked turnoff to the Cave of the Mounds, about three miles west of Mount Horeb.

The Cave of the Mounds, a National Natural Landmark, is in a valley to the left side of County F and is available for tours. Charles Brigham discovered the cave in 1939 while he was quarrying limestone near his barn. The main cavern originated more than a million years ago as acidic water dripped down from the surface and gradually dissolved the

A Silver Crested Polish hen named
Sarafina is one of many unusual
animals on the Moen Creek Cottage
Farm. Owner Linda Derrickson has
found that each animal has a
"distinct personality," and they
are all given names.

Tour guide Tom Rygh, in traditional Norwegian clothing, poses
in front of the main house at Little
Norway.

A VIEW OF BLUE MOUNDS UNFOLDS FROM THE EAST TOWER AT BLUE MOUND STATE PARK.

underlying rock. After pausing there, continue north on County F which skirts the eastern edge of the town of Blue Mounds. Look for the blue-gray ridge of Blue Mounds State Park to the west. At 1,719 feet above sea level, the wooded park is atop the highest point in southern Wisconsin. To drive over to the park, venture into Blue Mounds on County ID and pick up Mounds Park Road. On a park visit, climb up one of the two forty-foot lookout towers for a magnificent view.

Sticking to County F, instead of detouring to the state facility, pass Dane County's Brigham Park about a mile and a half north of Blue Mounds. This park rests on a high hill overlooking a valley, which stretches about thirty-five miles north to the Wisconsin River. From this vantage point, the low humps of the Baraboo Range can be seen. Contour strip farming in the valley adds to the landscape's delightful spring palette, as the deep earth tones hopscotch from a rich ebony of newly turned earth to a soft jade-green pastureland. Brigham Park contains one of Wisconsin's few remaining natural stands of mature sugar maples. The maples flourish in the hilltop's fertile north-slope soil, as they are well watered in the damp environment. Fog and rains have protected the trees from the prairie fires that regularly scoured the valley below in pre-pioneer days.

Continue northward on County F toward Black Earth, past the scattering of neat farms and country churches. Pause to reflect on the passage of life and time at a pioneer cemetery about eight miles north of Blue Mounds. On the north side of the road is a marker noting that the first parish in the area, St. Simon, was formed here in 1860. A second church was built on the site in 1883, honoring St. James. That building burned in 1969 and all that remains is a rusty red pump under a wind-bent pine whose needles whisper a hymn to the spring sun.

FRANK LLOYD WRIGHT COUNTRY

THE ROUTE

Drive south on Wisconsin Highway 23 from Spring Green to County Road T. Follow T southeast to Barneveld.

There are ghosts along the Wisconsin River. Their spirit feet dangle in the cooling, willow-draped shallows near Sweet Island, just off Wisconsin Highway 23. You hear them in the prairie grass alongside Lowery Creek, which gurgles past the old Jones farm. They walk the rows of corn fronting Coon Rock Road, a soft passing that causes each golden stalk to polka. They're overhead, lazily soaring on the updraft of Wyoming Valley. The spirits brush the walls of Taliesin, architect Frank Lloyd Wright's home and studio. During the noon Angelus, the ghosts bow assembled heads in prayer in the graveyard behind Unity Chapel on narrow Iowa County Road T. And when the moon shines, the ghosts mischievously tickle the broad black-and-white sides of dozing Holsteins.

Spring Green is where these apparitions gather on busy tourism weekends, drifting in from the surrounding countryside to rest quietly at the junction of U.S. Highway 14 and Wisconsin Highway 23. There, they watch the tourists arrive from Madison and points beyond. The town's galleries, restaurants, and stores provide a contemporary electricity to a one-time

THE WRIGHT STUFF

FRANK LLOYD WRIGHT MAY BE ONE OF WISCONSIN'S MOST FAMOUS SONS.

Noted architect Frank Lloyd Wright was born on June 8, 1867, in Richland Center, Wisconsin. In his teens, he settled down in Madison to attend the University of Wisconsin and study civil engineering. Wanting to live in a larger city, Wright eventually left school after two years and moved to Chicago to work as a draftsman in an engineering office. While there, he designed and built homes for wealthy clients of the company. He soon moved out on his own and over the next twenty years became one of the best-known architects in the country.

Wright died on April 9, 1959, leaving behind an influential architectural legacy. Foremost was his original building style, called "organic architecture." He loved low, sweeping roofs that hung over walls and windows, and he often incorporated a Far Eastern look into his structures. Among his most famous designs is that of the S. C. Johnson Wax Administrative Building in Racine, Wisconsin.

Although he traveled around the world, he always called Wisconsin his home. Taliesin East, where he built his house, school, and studio, is in Spring Green near his beloved Wisconsin River.

railway village. Spring Green was born in 1856, with the laying of track for the Milwaukee and Mississippi Railroad, and it quickly became a prosperous farm town.

Park and stroll the town streets to touch this past. Along the tracks is a railway station converted into a bank, plus two cheese warehouses now containing shops. One of the dignified old white buildings on Washington Street houses the Wisconsin Artists Showcase in the Jura Silverman Gallery. This hobbit house is a happy jumble of oil paintings, intricate weavings, pottery, glassware, sculpture, and jewelry. Downtown, you'll find St. John's Catholic Church on Jefferson Street, with its Wright-influenced exterior, and dim, incense-fragranced interior. A marvelous window there was designed by an artist from Taliesin Architects, which has its drafting studio in Wright's Hillside School, just outside Spring Green. Other town buildings have a Wright-influenced, flat-roof look.

Frank Lloyd Wright's spirit is strongest at Taliesin, a National Historic Landmark. The visitor center, its Riverview Terrace Cafe, gallery, and bookshop are located at the intersection of Highway 23 and County Road C. From there, you take buses to the main complex of Wright buildings, ten minutes to the west amid six hundred acres of farmland. Here, Wright's truism, "Own your own view," still solidly rings. No cars, other than for clients coming to the architectural studio, are allowed at Taliesin proper.

There are other sites of interest to explore in Spring Green as well. After touring the Wright area, drive to the American Players Theater by following the signs just beyond the House on the Rock Resort at County C

AMERICAN PLAYERS THEATER IS ONE OF THE MOST POPULAR OUTDOOR CLASSICAL THEATERS IN THE COUNTRY.

LEFT:

A SOLEMN TOMBSTONE STANDS IN THE CEMETERY AT FRANK LLOYD WRIGHT'S UNITY CHAPEL.

BELOW:

FRANK LLOYD WRIGHT'S TALIESIN NEAR SPRING GREEN IS A PERFECT EXAMPLE OF HIS ORGANIC ARCHITECTURE.

and Golf Course Road east of Highway 23. Located on 110 acres of hills and forests, the outdoor theater has presented Shakespeare, Molière, Chekhov, Wilde, and other playwriting greats since 1980. You can casually picnic prior to the productions, which run from mid June through the first week of October.

There are more ghosts on Iowa County Road C as it edges north, drifting through the seventy-seven-acre Tower Hill State Park and the abandoned town of Helena. The village died out after being bypassed by the railroad in 1857 in favor of nearby Spring Green. All that now remains are several limestone building foundations and a reconstructed shot tower. The wooden tower, used to make lead shot for muskets, sits atop a sandstone bluff overlooking the river. Construction on the original shot tower in what is now Tower Hill State Park began in 1831 by men using crowbars and pickaxes. They dug a vertical shaft 120 feet down through the bluff and then added a 90-foot-long tunnel leading to the edge of the Wisconsin River. Lead was secured through mines in the area and melted at the top of the tower. The molten metal was poured through screens and hardened on the way to the bottom of the shaft, becoming spherical on its plunge to a pool of water. The shot was then hauled out of the tunnel, sorted, packaged, and hauled away.

Bid goodbye to Spring Green's ghosts and move on. From Highway 23, take County Road T to the south, the turnoff for which is to the left just beyond the river and the Wright visitor center. After about six miles or so, as T winds its southeasterly way, you need to take a short jog south for about a quarter mile on County Road H to again pick up T. Watch carefully for the road signs, or you might miss the second turn; Duesler Creek is to the left as you negotiate this little twitch. Then continue southeast again on County T, which passes the Trout Creek State Fishery Area, a sprawling conservation project funded by the sale of state trout stamps. The road here has narrow shoulders, not leaving much room for avoiding oncoming traffic. At tiny Birch Lake, about another two miles down the road, there is a multiple purpose dam that was built in 1964 to provide flood control as well as a fishing site.

After passing a picnic shelter, ball field, and playground, you'll ascend a relatively steep hill and enter the north side of Barneveld. The town, which lies along U.S. Highway 18 some twenty-five miles west of Madison, was heavily damaged during a tornado on June 8, 1984. Only the town water tower, a church, and several homes remained after the rampaging storm claimed nine lives and swept away the business district. So, there are more ghosts to contend with here. But now, even they are quiet as they stroll Barneveld's rebuilt streets, proud of its new facade.

NEW GLARUS

Driving through the stunning countryside of South Central Wisconsin's Green County is enough to make a sane man yodel. This is bucolic cheese and cow territory with limestone-rich pastures that are home to many of the state's largest dairy farms. Farmers around here have taken their cattle and milk seriously since the late 1860s.

But it's not all work and no play around here. Every other September, Monroe hosts the Cheesemaker's Ball at Cheese Days, a tradition sparked in 1914. Anyone tiring of street dancing during the festival can hop a motor coach for a tour of several local dairy plants. Samples of cheese are usually provided at each stop.

After getting your fill of cheese, drive north on Wisconsin Highway 69, pausing in Monticello where the Zwingli United Church of Christ—named after the stern Swiss religious reformer and patriot of the sixteenth century, Ulrich Zwingli—stands in stark greeting.

While in Monticello, pause for a Wisconsin-brewed Huber beer in the dim interior of Zipper's bar. Outside are pickups, their axles sitting low under loads of newly purchased rolls of bailing wire and one-hundred-pound bags of chicken feed. Drop in for supper at the M&M Cafe, the Monticello House, or the Raven's Bar & Grille. Gempeler's Supermarket is home of the richly spiced, homemade Alpine Boy Sausage.

Then it's back out to Highway 69, past the flower-festooned village park at the junction with Green County Road F, and the straight shot five miles north to New Glarus via the state roadway. The town was founded in 1845 by 108 hardy Swiss émigrés from the Canton of Glarus who were attracted to Wisconsin by the detailed reports sent back by a scouting party.

New Glarus definitely has charm, with its Swiss-chalet-like storefronts and window boxes exploding with geraniums in the red and white Swiss national colors. The annual Heidi Festival, which started in 1964, is a June celebration of Swiss culture and folklore replete with flag throwing and alpine horn blowing. A play, held in the high school auditorium, celebrates the story of Heidi, the little girl who journeyed to the Alps to live with her grandfather. And during the Wilhelm Tell Festival at the end of every summer since 1938, volunteers have staged a production in honor of the Swiss folk hero who shot the apple from his trusting son's head. The play is presented in German and English in the town's outdoor amphitheater.

New Glarus is a walker's town, with a required stop at the Chalet of the Golden Fleece Museum. This site was once the home of Edwin Barlow, the originator of the Wilhelm Tell drama, who packed his house with artifacts collected on jaunts around the world. Downtown, the Swiss Historical Village preserves New Glarus's pioneer heritage in its fourteen historic buildings.

THE ROUTE

Drive north on Wisconsin Highway 69 from Monroe to New Glarus.

BIKES ARE FOR RENT ALONG THE
SUGAR RIVER BIKE TRAIL IN NEW
GLARUS. THE TWENTY-THREE-MILE
TRAIL RUNS FROM NEW GLARUS TO
BRODHEAD WITH VIRTUALLY NO GRADE,
MAKING IT AN IDEAL TRACK FOR A
CASUAL BICYCLE RIDE.

CLOTHING FROM SWITZERLAND,
GERMANY, NORWAY, AND SCOTLAND
ARE SHOWN AT THE ANNUAL ETHNIC
FASHION SHOW AS PART OF NEW
GLARUS'S WILHELM TELL FESTIVAL.
HADEN BOWIE, SMILING, ON THE RIGHT,
WEARS A REPRODUCTION OF AN
USHERETTE COSTUME FROM THE SWISS
CANTON (STATE) OF APPENZELL; JACK
ROBERTS ALSO WEARS AUTHENTIC
SWISS CLOTHING.

A FULL MOON RISES OVER THE SNOWY CORNFIELDS NEAR DALEYVILLE.

Restaurants here specialize in hearty Old World fare. The kitchen of the New Glarus Hotel is run by Hans Lenzlingher, a native of St. Gallen, Switzerland. He specializes in *schnitzel* (breaded pork or veal cutlet), *roesti* (hash brown potatoes with onions and Swiss cheese), *kalberwurst* (veal sausage), *spaetzle* (a dumpling which can be prepared either by pan-frying or boiling the dough), and *bienenstich* (a sweet dough dessert coated in a honey almond glaze and Bavarian cream filling).

New Glarus is also known for its beer. The New Glarus Brewery opened in June 1993 and has won a barrel of awards for its twelve varieties of fine-tasting brews. It produces about nine thousand barrels of beer per year. The brewery's Hometown Blonde is an Old World–style pilsner, "delicate in appearance but with a backbone," while its Spotted Cow is a light ale made with flaked barley and Wisconsin malt that is naturally cloudy, since the yeast remains in the bottle.

After exploring the town, there are several opportunities to enjoy the region's natural beauty. Drive to nearby 305-acre New Glarus Woods State Park, six miles south of New Glarus, via Wisconsin Highway 39/69. The heavily wooded park is bisected by the roller-coaster ride of Green County Road NN, which was originally a muddy trail used by the military during the Black Hawk War of 1832. The park is a half-mile west of Highway 69 on the north side of County N.

The Sugar River State Trail traverses 23.5 miles of green countryside between New Glarus and Brodhead to the southeast. The path, which lies along an abandoned railway bed, rolls along the banks of the Sugar River through the state-managed Albany Wildlife Area and the villages of Monticello and Albany. Trail headquarters is in a century-old depot in downtown New Glarus. Among the trail services, which include rental bikes and bathrooms, is a shuttle service that can pick up tired cyclists and hikers along the trail.

There's more smooth biking possible in Green County along the aptly named Cheese Country Recreational Trail, which begins nine miles east of Monroe and runs forty-seven miles west to Mineral Point. The path is well named because it traverses the cow-cluttered countryside along the old Milwaukee Road railroad tracks through Green, Lafayette, and Iowa Counties. A dedicated cyclist will eventually cross fifty-six overpasses and a 449-foot-high bridge over the sluggish Pecatonica River south of Browntown. ATVs and horses also use this trail, one of the few in the state to allow such varied use. The corridor runs along segments of prairie plantings, with songbirds nesting everywhere.

For extra backcountry driving, take an alternate route from New Glarus. Pick up Green County Road N just west the state forest and go north to connect with County H, a leafy cathedral thoroughfare leading to Blanchardville ten miles to the northwest. You can also explore Rustic

Road 81—a 2.9-mile paved stretch also called Marty Road that runs northwest between County H and Highway 39. This roadway scoots across the top of a craggy ridge where daisies, buffalo grass, coneflowers, sorrel, and wild roses explode from the ditches; cardinals and woodpeckers zoom back and forth; and well-kept, turn-of-the-nineteenth-century farmhouses lie along the route, their white porches wide and inviting. As you drive through the invigorating New Glarus countryside, windows down, remember to practice your yodeling, and it will soon feel like home.

PART V

THE SOUTHEAST:
LAND OF WOODS AND WATER

FACING PAGE:
A GNARLY BURR OAK TREE STANDS ON THE SCUPPERNONG SPRINGS TRAIL IN THE KETTLE MORAINE SOUTHERN UNIT.

ABOVE:
MARSH GRASS REFLECTS ON THE WATER OF CROOKED LAKE.

Lake Michigan is the third largest of the Great Lakes and the only one located entirely within the continental United States. Its cooling waters make up the entire eastern border of Wisconsin. The lake, at 22,400 square miles, is a prime recreation locale for boaters, both of the sail and power variety. Fisherfolk also flock to Lake Michigan for charter cruises, eager for a day of questing after German browns, lake trout, and salmon.

Most of the communities along the water sport well-designed harbors to accommodate these freshwater fans, with amenities ranging from fish-cleaning stations to restaurants and parks. There is hardly a better way to spend a sunny summer weekend than lolling on the lake with friends, as burgers are grilling on-board and refreshing brew is served.

Southeast Wisconsin is also a land of woods, with its north and south units of the Kettle Moraine State Forest to explore. The backroads throughout this glacial landscape are perfect for admiring autumn's changing leaves or for providing quick access to muscle-stretching biking and hiking paths. Large portions of the state's Ice Age Trail wander through each forest section, as part of the 1,000-mile-long system that traces the outermost edges of the glaciers' ancient course.

In this corner of Wisconsin, the determined traveler can walk down a dusty road into history near the town of Eagle at Old World Wisconsin. The museum complex is comprised of nineteenth-century buildings collected from around the state. Another brush with the past is also possible at the Old Wade House in Greenbush, where a Civil War reenactment each autumn brings alive the not-so-good-old days.

But for fast contemporary times, Road America at Elkhart Lake reverberates to the rumble of throaty engines throughout the car-racing season. The world's top drivers compete along the convoluted course that roller-coasters through the Kettle Moraine world. Who knows who might be in the crowd of spectators—racing fan Paul Newman is a regular there.

It's easy to be a regular visitor in Wisconsin.

FOND DU LAC AND GREEN LAKE COUNTIES

Spring in Green Lake County and western Fond du Lac County brings the debut of trillium in a purple and white post-Easter blush. The wet earth sprawls open to the season's sun, with polka-dot puddles on its winter-smudged face. The rough afternoon waters of Green Lake are ocean-like, stirred by a brisk nor'wester over the cornfields, and the waves stampede against the small sandy beach and rock rifle along the shore. The major arteries through this region include the east-west Wisconsin Highways 23 and 44 and the north-south Wisconsin Highways 73 and 49. They are joined by country roads that hopscotch their way around Green and Puckaway Lakes.

Drive through this vista to reach Ripon, about two miles east of the border between Fond du Lac and Green Lake Counties. Ripon College looks

THE ROUTE

Take Wisconsin Highway 23 west from Fond du Lac to reach Ripon. Continue west on 23 to Wisconsin Highway 49; drive north on 49 to Berlin. From there, take County Road F west to County Road D; follow D south to Rustic Road 22 (White River Road), which runs southwest to reconnect with D. County D will then lead you southwest to Princeton. Follow D as it runs south and east; jog north on Wisconsin Highway 73 to pick up County Road K near the western shore of Green Lake. Drive east on K to County Road A, which runs north to the town of Green Lake.

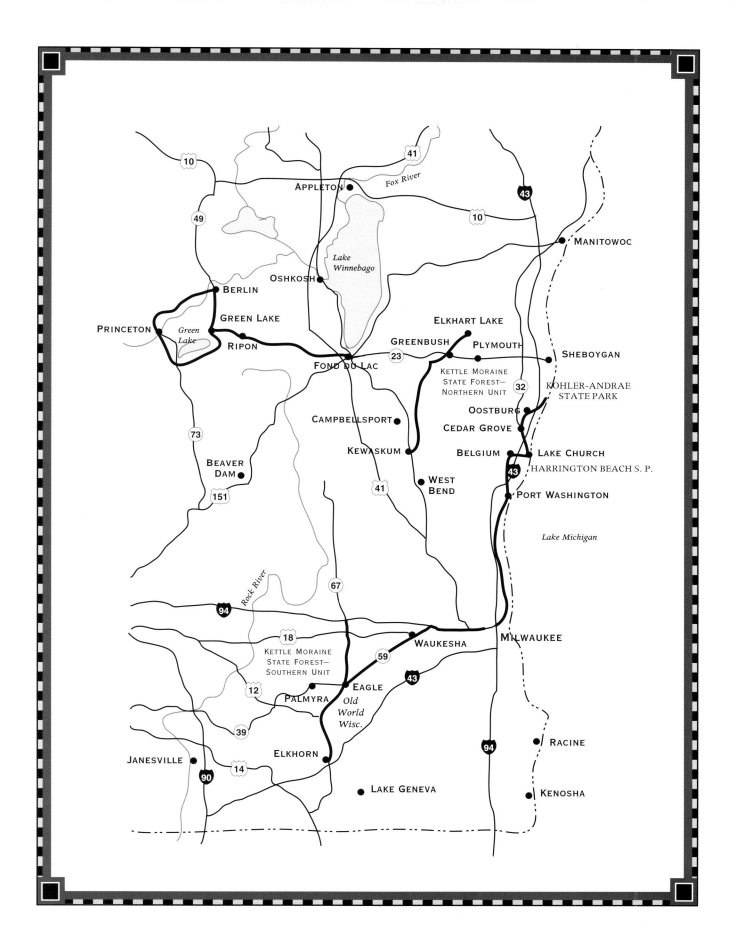

A PARK BENCH
PROVIDES A GRAND
VIEW OF THE
GREEN LAKE COUNTY
COURTHOUSE.

FACING PAGE, TOP:
HOLIDAY LIGHTS SHINE OUTSIDE THE HOME OF DANIEL TRAMPF IN RIPON.

FACING PAGE, BOTTOM:
TREES REFLECT OFF THE WATER OF GREEN LAKE AT SUNRISE.

down on the city from a bluff, its classic buildings exuding an aura of permanence. Among its many distinguished alums over the years is noted actor Harrison Ford.

After a jaunt from Ripon to Berlin, with its numerous antique shops, take County Road F west over to County Road D to skirt the bird-rich White River Marsh State Wildlife Area. White River Road, a 5.5-mile section of the state's Rustic Road system, cuts through the reserve, edging south to D. Mostly gravel, the narrow back lane crosses two wide concrete bridges. Low-lying groves of birch and aspen quake in the breeze along the route, their first buds quivering when tossed about by the wind. Princeton pops out of the earth on a bend of the seasonally swollen Fox River. The downtown's grand old buildings have been refurbished to within an inch of their original snappiness. Trendy restaurants and overflowing antique shops bear witness that tourism is one of Green Lake County's economic mainstays. From Princeton, drive south on County D, to pick up Highway 73 at Green Lake Terrace on the west end of Green Lake. After less than a mile on Highway 73, take County K, which swings around the south shore of the lake. The paved road passes picturesque Blackbird Point and Spring and Twin Lakes to the junction with County Road A, where a turn north leads to the town of Green Lake.

Green Lake has been a getaway mecca since the early 1900s. As such, it's probably the only place in the state where you can have a trophy bass taxidermied and purchase a bottle of quality champagne in the same store.

GRAND OLD PARTY PUTS DOWN ITS ROOTS

A small white schoolhouse in Ripon, Wisconsin, is a GOP shrine, as well as a National Historic Landmark. Fifty-three voters met here in 1854 to discuss the formation of a new political party. The idea for the assembly had come about at least two years earlier, when newspaper editor Horace Greeley met with Alvan Earle Bovary of Ripon to push for the dissolution of the Whig Party to unite anti-slavery elements in the country. Bovary suggested the name "Republican" for the new party because it "was a good name, one with charm and prestige," he said.

Bovary later recalled, "We went to the little meeting. Whigs, Free Soilers, and Democrats. We came out Republicans, and were the first Republicans in the Union."

The building, called simply the Little White Schoolhouse, is now a museum.

THE LITTLE WHITE SCHOOLHOUSE, REPORTED TO BE THE BIRTHPLACE OF THE REPUBLICAN PARTY, IS PICTURED HERE IN RIPON IN THE EARLY 1900S. TODAY IT IS A NATIONAL HISTORIC LANDMARK. (WISCONSIN HISTORICAL SOCIETY, WHI (S65) 93)

Trasher's Opera House downtown has been the area's cultural center since it was built in 1910. The old white hall is now the home base for the Green Lake Festival of Music each July and retains its elegant charm for parties, jazz concerts, and old-movie showings.

Illinois Avenue, along the south side of the lake, showcases a democratic blend of large mansions and cozy summer homes. The Heidel House, a major resort here, opened its doors on New Year's Eve in 1945. The original manor was a private residence when it was built in 1890. In 1989, an adjoining mansion once owned by a member of the Swift Meat Packing family of Chicago was converted into the Grey Rock Mansion gourmet restaurant.

Green Lake is not just for layabouts content with sailboating, swimming, golfing, horseback riding, and concert going. There's also the annual chili cook-off on the Saturday after Labor Day. Winner of the event attends the national cook-off in California.

Even with all the twenty-first-century happenings on its fringes, the lake here remains content with itself. Its depth ranges from 257 feet at the Head of the Lake on the southwest side, to a mere ten feet or so at Pleasant Point on the northeast. About 220 springs feed the lake, keeping it fresh and clear for the resident bluegills. As you stand on its shores and reflect on the day, you may feel contentment as well.

KETTLE MORAINE FOREST—NORTHERN UNIT

Over the centuries, glaciers enthusiastically rearranged the Wisconsin landscape. Almost the entire state became a geological jumble during the Ice Age, and today rocky debris can be seen throughout the Kettle Moraine Forest—Northern Unit, which is primarily in Sheboygan County. A kettle is a depression in the ground that was caused by glacial ice melting. As the glaciers melted, they often left behind huge chunks of ice buried under the earth. When the ice thawed, the surface cover collapsed to form a dip that reminded early settlers of a cooking pot or "kettle." A moraine is a rough ridge of rubble that marked the outermost rim of a glacier.

This landscape provides great challenges for outdoor fun—even simply driving through the region always brings a breath of fresh air. Since 1936, state acquisitions have protected much of the land from developers. This section of the larger Kettle Moraine State Forest, which also consists of a southern unit, covers 29,000 acres that spread thirty miles throughout Sheboygan, Fond du Lac, and Washington Counties. The forest carpets the landscape between Glenbeulah in the north and Kewaskum in the south as part of the state's Ice Age National Scientific Reserve, established in 1971 to protect and interpret Wisconsin's glacial geography.

This region is easily accessed from Milwaukee by taking Interstate 43 north to Wisconsin Highway 57, which leads directly into Plymouth on the eastern edge of the forest, or by taking Wisconsin Highway 45 north from Milwaukee and driving through Germantown, West Bend, and on to

THE ROUTE

Beginning in Kewaskum, follow the marked signs of the Kettle Moraine Forest Scenic Drive north through the forest to Greenbush. From there, take County Road A northeast to Elkhart Lake.

ABOVE:
THE KETTLE MORAINE DRIVE, SEEN HERE FROM THE ICE AGE NATIONAL SCENIC TRAIL, IS LINED WITH TALL TREES.

RIGHT:
A SPRING BUD SPROUTS ALONGSIDE THE ICE AGE NATIONAL SCENIC TRAIL.

UNION ARMY SOLDIERS TIP THEIR HATS IN A SALUTE TO VICTORY AFTER A CIVIL WAR REENACTMENT AT THE OLD WADE HOUSE.

LEFT:
CROOKED LAKE IS NESTLED IN THE KETTLE MORAINE STATE FOREST'S NORTHERN UNIT.

Kewaskum. You can also reach the area from Sheboygan via Wisconsin Highway 23 west to Plymouth, or from Sheboygan Falls via County Road C west.

The twenty-five-mile-long Kettle Moraine Scenic Drive leads you into the most stunning parts of the forest along a succession of winding county roads. But don't worry if you miss one of the signs along the marked route and end up on another course. They all are wonderfully scenic. Highlights along the system include the Greenbush Recreation Area, Moraine Ridge Trail, Long Lake Nature Trail, and Mauthe Lake Recreation Area. Excellent fishing opportunities abound in many of these areas, especially on Mauthe Lake, 8.5 miles from Campbellsport, or Long Lake, with its 417 acres of walleye and perch waiting to be taken. Crooked Lake covers 91 acres, with private cottages available for rent along the shoreline.

The forest's extensive 133-mile system of trails is great whether for cross-country skiing in winter or trekking in summer. There are also fifty-eight miles of marked snowmobile trails in the forest. For skiers, the best season lasts from eight to twelve weeks, usually from December through early spring.

A must stop on your Kettle Moraine drive is the Henry S. Reuss Ice Age Interpretive Center along Wisconsin Highway 67. The hilltop site is eight miles southwest of Plymouth and just south of the Long Lake Nature Trail—but about two miles north of the Zillmer Hiking and Ski Trail. The information center overlooks the heart of the Kettle Moraine countryside where you can stand on the wide observation deck for an impressive view of several glacially formed ridges and peaks.

As you pause on a leaf-littered path that cuts through the state forest, time becomes irrelevant. These rocks have been around for a long, long time. One exceptional section of the Ice Age Trail in the Kettle Moraine is a 2.6-mile, two-hour leg that loops over rough terrain. Look for wild turkeys peeking over the grass tops and soaring turkey vultures.

There are two entry points to this part of the trail. The first is on the south end of the trail, along Sheboygan County Road U, but the best is on Highway 67, about 1.5 miles west of Sheboygan County Road A. Up a small rise in an open field on the south side of the highway is a gravel patch well away from the road for a convenient pullover.

Some of the Kettle Moraine Scenic Drive's backroads are less than smooth, but imagine bouncing in a stagecoach over a rutted dirt and plank highway for endless hours,

THE WADE HOUSE WAS A STAGECOACH STOP BETWEEN SHEBOYGAN AND FOND DU LAC IN THE MID 1800S.

banging elbows and shoulders with your fellow passengers. Add the dust in hot, dry weather and the bone-chilling cold in winter and you have 1850s travel in Wisconsin. Today, thank heavens, the roads around the Old Wade House in northeastern Wisconsin's Kettle Moraine are paved. The inn offered good food, clean bath water, and a comfortable place in which to sleep for nineteenth-century travelers tough enough for the arduous forty-mile journey between Sheboygan on the Lake Michigan shore and inland Fond du Lac. Now a state historical site, the facility is seven miles west of Plymouth, just off Highway 23 in the hamlet of Greenbush. The stagecoach stop was also an assembly point for Wisconsin troops during the Civil War, which makes it appropriate to use as a battlefield for a Civil War reenactment each autumn.

For a quieter afternoon, move north from Greenbush along County A, on any one in a warren of narrow county roads that dip through the tree-covered landscape. Where all these roads converge, you'll discover Elkhart Lake, a resort community since the late nineteenth century. Today, the fastest action is found at Road America on Highway 67, two miles south of Elkhart Lake where modifieds and formula racecars whip around the white-knuckle, four-mile, fourteen-turn course. Snuggled amid 525 acres of rolling, oak-blanketed hills, Road America is enjoyed by locals, visitors, and other personalities—like film star Paul Newman—who come to watch the racing and be ogled themselves.

There are many other county sideroads to explore around the Kettle Moraine State Forest–Northern Unit. One of the best alternate routes is along Sheboygan County Roads S and A, which cut along the east side of the forest. Another exemplary route can be found along Sheboygan County Road C north of Wisconsin Highway 23 at Glenbeulah.

Another fine trek off the main Kettle Moraine Scenic Drive runs from the maple-shrouded County Road DD south from Highway 67 to the crossroads of New Fane at the junction with County Road S. The winding road meanders past Buttermilk Lake, along a cross-country ski trail, and around the Chip 'n Chatter Nature Trail. Yet another good route is County Road U, which edges east from Highway 67 to County A. At the junction of U and A is the Parnell Tower, a lofty observation post high astride one of the area's tallest hills.

THE LAKE MICHIGAN SHORELINE

A jaunt north from Milwaukee opens a new world. Several picturesque routes will lead you to the town of Port Washington, on the bluffs overlooking Lake Michigan. The port city was founded in 1835 and now serves as a marina for private pleasure boats. Our route follows rural Ozaukee County Road C, north of Mequon, which runs along the shoreline, through the ever-dwindling farmland, and past sprawling housing estates before edging directly into downtown Port Washington. Upper Lake Park along Lake Street offers a great vista of the town and lake. To get to the park,

THE ROUTE

From the Milwaukee area, take Interstate 43/Wisconsin Highway 32 north and exit at County Road C; jog east on County Road T to pick up Lake Shore Road, which runs north to rejoin C. Follow County C into Port Washington. From there, take County Road KW north to County Road D in the town of Belgium. Drive east on D to Harrington Beach State Park. Drive north from the park on Sauk Trail Road, making stops at Cedar Grove and Oostburg via county roads. At the intersection of Sauk Trail Road and County Road KK, turn east to reach the Kohler-Andrae State Park.

A nature trail winds through the dunes at Kohler-Andrae State Park.

Did someone say lunch? The working farm "Llamas of Bahr Creek" on Sauk Trail Road encourages visitors.

An abandoned sand castle sits impressively on the shore of Lake Michigan at Harrington Beach State Park.

drive through Veterans Memorial Park along the lakeshore north of downtown.

An alternate route takes you on a forty-five-minute drive directly from the city center of Milwaukee to Port Washington via Interstate 43/Wisconsin Highway 32. Parallel the Lake Michigan shoreline as much as possible with a good state map or county maps showing the sideroads. From 43/32, exit at the Highway 32 off-ramp (No. 93) north. Highway 32 is named after the famed Red Arrow Division, a heroic Army National Guard unit from the upper Midwest. Note the division logo on the highway marker signs: a red arrow piercing a line, signifying the unit smashing through the enemy's defenses. On Highway 32, drive east about seven miles, aiming for the twin smokestacks of the Wisconsin Electric Power Company.

Shopping aficionados in Port Washington love the summer sausages at Bernie's Fine Meats and the biscotti, scones, mini-creampuffs, and focaccia at Oma's Breads. The bakers at Sweetheart Cakes work all night preparing wonderful cookies and tea cakes. For comfort food, Harry's Restaurant has been a staple here since it opened in 1936.

Now hit the next stop, a pause in Belgium, about ten minutes north of Port Washington. There, emerald-colored hearts on the hamlet's welcome signs show off the locals' Luxembourgian ties. On the second Sunday of August, Belgium honors its heritage with a brassy parade and polka dancing. Other Luxembourgers emigrated to nearby Fredonia, Holy Cross, Dacada, and Lake Church.

On the eastern side of Exit 107 off Interstate 43 on County D, pause for a prayer in the wind-tousled cemetery behind St. Mary's Church while on the way to Harrington Beach State Park. The 637-acre park, only ten miles north of Port Washington, was originally a limestone quarry. What remains after the rock was removed is a fifty-foot-deep, 26-acre lake ringed by a spiderweb of hiking trails. After the quarry was closed in 1925, various owners lived on the land, and in 1968 Wisconsin took it over to make the park—named after the late E. L. Harrington, a popular superintendent of the old Wisconsin Conservation Commission.

After leaving Harrington Beach State Park, cross from Ozaukee County into Sheboygan County by driving north on Sauk Trail Road. This tidy Dutch country has fifth generation families that still own their ancestors' neat farms. Walvoord, Hoftiener, Smies, Risseeuw, and Weedmans Roads now attest to this longtime Dutch presence. Turn west on Amsterdam Road from Sauk Trail Road and drive about 1.5 miles to Highway 32. This route leads to Cedar Grove, a village settled by pioneers from Zeeland, a low-lying area on the Dutch coast. Thick lake mist contributes to the area's lush grass, which is loved by happy Holsteins and Guernseys. A bell-ringing town crier marches through Cedar Grove on the last Friday and Saturday in July to announce the town's Holland Festival, where there are parades and street scrubbing to impress the tourists and races for kids wearing clunky wooden shoes.

While cows are in the majority here, more-exotic animals can be found on several farms along Sauk Trail Road. Mark and Brigitte DeMaster and their family have been raising llamas on their property since the late 1980s. The animals are welcome for their lean meat and their prized wool.

After Cedar Grove comes the Dutch community of Oostburg, reached by driving north on Highway 32 to County Road A, which runs east into town. The bedroom community serves Sheboygan, about six miles to the north, and Milwaukee some forty miles to the south.

Kohler-Andrae State Park, a thirty-minute drive north of Harrington Beach near the Black River Wildlife Reserve, is a favorite hiking locale. To get there from Oostburg, drive east a half-mile on Sheboygan County Road AA and return to Sauk Trail Road, which angles to the northeast and quickly parallels Interstate 43. After about three miles, Sheboygan County Road KK is seen. Turn east on KK and cross the freeway, driving directly to Old Park Road for the entrance to the joint state parks. Ancient people constructed fantastic mounds shaped like eagles and other sacred animals throughout this area. After these people faded away, the Ottawa, Menominee, Ho-Chunk, and Sauk moved here, attracted by an abundance of game fish, shelter, and fresh water.

In 1927, a local property owner donated 122 acres of pine-studded dunes to the state to be called Terry Andrae State Park in honor of her husband. In 1966, a 280-acre memorial parcel was added in honor of Sheboygan business leader John Michael Kohler. The state has since purchased another 600 acres, making the combined parks total about 1,000 acres.

An easy two-hour hike north on the Kohler Dunes Cordwalk extends 2.5 miles along the Lake Michigan shoreline. The wooden walkway is embedded atop the dunes for a wind-blown vantage point of the lake. Stay on the cordwalk, because walking in the dunes causes erosion. Park at the lot near the Visitor Information Center, where the trail starts to the north. For a shorter hike, enjoy the 1.5-mile Woodland Dunes Nature Trail. The nearby surf provides a musical undercurrent to the soft whispering of the ever-moving pine branches.

KETTLE MORAINE FOREST —SOUTHERN UNIT

Imagine a towering ice sheet—a mile high in some places—that once covered southeastern Wisconsin. When this huge glacier melted, it dumped a trail of rubble across the region. Today, mounds of pebbles and pumpkin-sized rocks are sprinkled in that spot, with individual boulders tossed here and streambeds twisted there. To see these glacial remains, drive through the Kettle Moraine State Forest–Southern Unit, via Wisconsin Highway 67. The woods roll along to the south, incorporating 18,000 diverse acres of rolling hills, wetlands, prairies, and deep kettles in chunks of Jefferson, Waukesha, and Walworth Counties.

THE ROUTE

Take Wisconsin Highway 67 south from Interstate 94 to Elkhorn, through the Kettle Moraine State Forest–Southern Unit.

A snowy trail runs through the Kettle Moraine Southern Unit.

County Road Z parallels a green field in the Kettle Moraine Southern Unit.

The Kettle Moraine Southern Unit has several amazing geological formations, with the most impressive being the landmark Stone Elephant, which measures thirty-nine feet in diameter. To find the Elephant, park at the Bald Bluff Scenic Overlook and Natural Area on County Road H, a minute or so north of Young Road. From there, walk along the Ice Age Trail to pick up the path to the rock.

Other natural wonders can be found in this area as well. Off Highway 67, three miles north of the intersection with Wisconsin Highway 59, is an ancient glacial lake bed that was once forty feet deep; a giant kettle can be spotted on County H, almost a mile north of the intersection with U.S. Highway 12; and La Grange Lake, near the marked Ice Age Trail where it crosses U.S. 12, is a shallow pool surrounded by marshland. The diversity of topography and ground formations makes this area a wonderful hostelry for all types of wild animals, such as the red fox. The Kettle Moraine is also one of the few places in Wisconsin to discover rare pasqueflowers, which bloom only in mid April.

Popular hiking trails in the Kettle Moraine include the Scuppernong Springs Natural Trail and the Rice Lake Nature Trail, as well as paths around the Scuppernong Marsh Wildlife Area, the Ottawa Lake Recreation Area, and La Grange Lake. There are more than thirty-four miles of hiking routes along the well-marked Scuppernong and McMiller trail systems, with the paths looped for simple access and exit.

The Emma F. Carlin Trail takes hikers and bikers along abandoned logging routes that cut deep into the heart of the forest. The trail system begins near Waukesha County Road Z, one mile south of Highway 59. Park in the lot off County Z and walk toward the trailhead. A large map carved on a wooden sign, which outlines the system, indicates the entryway. Be aware that there are steep slopes and plenty of S-curves along some of the paths, particularly on the Red Loop. Listen for the drumbeat of redheaded woodpeckers on the decaying stumps and watch for deer.

A variety of trail types can be found along the Nordic Ski and Hiking Trails, ranging from easy to extremely challenging. After the first steeply wooded hill, a panorama of meadowland sweeps off to the horizon where the occasional wild turkey can be seen strutting along. Spotted tail hawks and vultures circle the skies here on sunny days, and strikingly tall coneflowers, wild daisies, and brilliant orange poppies blanket the open slopes. The system is on Walworth County Road H about two miles south of Bluff Road, with the main trails six miles south of the village of Palmyra. Rest rooms are open at the trailhead. This system offers some of the best cross-country skiing in the Kettle Moraine.

The Ice Age Trail in the Southern Unit of the Kettle Moraine is part of the 1,000-mile-long span of hiking paths that reach far across Wisconsin's midsection, following the perimeter of the retreating glaciers. Park in the gravel lot where both the Ice Age Trail and the Horse Trail cross U.S. 12, with the lot on the north side of the highway near Sweno Road along

Stelbrook Creek. Orange and yellow markers indicate the trail, making it simple to find.

Watch for the steep ascents and drops on this route, as well as bare rocks and exposed roots. White and black oaks abound along the way, with their huge, twisted trunks straight from a hobbit-land of fantasy. Shagbark hickories pop out from the forest, and the silvery forms of quaking aspen are scattered around for visual variety. Deep purple violets and yellow buttercups provide a colorful Persian carpet of color during their appropriate blossoming seasons, and wild raspberries wait to be sampled when they are in the height of their mid-summer season.

A wetland once stretched for more than twenty miles off to the west of the Ice Age Trail toward today's village of Palmyra, but now only a few hundred acres of those once pristine scenes remain. Subdivisions and a scattering of faux mansions with wide lawns and pools have encroached on the landscape.

The Scuppernong Springs Trail lies across Waukesha County Road ZZ, accessible from the Ottawa Lake Recreation Area. A wooden boardwalk meanders across a pond where an earthen dam once blocked the Scuppernong River to create a fish holding area where trout were raised in the early 1900s. The remains of the nearby Scuppernong Springs Hotel are almost lost in overgrowth nearby.

The Kettle Moraine Forest's Whitewater Lake, Ottawa Lake, and Pinewoods recreational areas provide good overnight bases for outdoor adventures, whether they be hiking, biking, or fishing trips.

Wise anglers will find the best panfish waters in Whitewater, Lower Spring, Ottawa, and Rice Lakes. These lakes are also great for larger warmwater game fish, such as bass and northern pike. Bluff Creek is ace when it comes to fly-casting for trout. It is accessible via a fire lane off a small parking area on Hi-Lo Road in the far southern end of the forest between the Hickory Woods Group Campground and the Lone Tree Bluff Scenic and Historical Overlook.

The Kettle Moraine truly is a place of escape.

OLD WORLD WISCONSIN

The midday sun lies heavily on the narrow dirt road wending through Old World Wisconsin. Along the low ditches and vine-entwined split-rail fences, droning cicadas discuss the pending afternoon. A velvet breeze tickles acres of ripening wheat to the left, causing the heavy-headed stalks to perform a ballet. The grain is already transforming into a burnished ripening gold. On the right is a season-battered barn and farmhouse that have survived years of lashing spring rains, winter wind, and hot, cloudless summer skies.

Old World Wisconsin, owned and operated by the Wisconsin Historical Society, is an open-air museum with more than fifty pioneer

THE ROUTE

To get to Old World Wisconsin from Milwaukee, take Wisconsin Highway 59 west through Waukesha to connect with Wisconsin Highway 67 at Eagle. The site is about a mile south of Eagle on Highway 67.

ABOVE:
A SCARECROW STANDS
GUARD AT THE SCHULZ
FARM IN OLD WORLD
WISCONSIN.

RIGHT:
INTERPRETERS AT OLD
WORLD WISCONSIN
DRESS IN AUTHENTIC
CLOTHES OF THE
PERIOD. HERE,
SHARON HENSERSKY
MAKES AN ADJUSTMENT
TO HER BABUSHKA ON
THE PORCH OF THE
SCHULZ FARM.

Looking like ghosts on the wall, nightdresses hang in the southwest corner of the bedroom at the Schuttler farm at Old World Wisconsin. The farm was built in 1875.

buildings that have been gathered from around the state and refurbished. The site was founded in 1976 as the state's major bicentennial project and is located 1.5 miles south of Eagle, Wisconsin. Eagle is in the heart of the Kettle Moraine State Forest–Southern Unit, thirty-five miles south and west from Milwaukee and seventy-five miles north of Chicago.

Footsteps kick up dust as visitors to this state historical site step into Wisconsin's pioneer heritage. Cars are *verboten* here and a rural road remains just that. The outdoors is bathed in an unsanitized perfume of pungent wildflowers and manure of penned cattle. Strolling along Old World's two-and-a-half-mile route today makes the long-ago world of early Wisconsin settlers come alive again.

It's a half-mile to the Rankinen log house from the parking lot—an easy fifteen-minute stroll. It doesn't take long before coming to a path that leads to the weathered old slab-sided home. The beams are huge but carefully notched and chinked against the weather. If you prefer not to walk, tractor-pulled wagons take visitors around the grounds. Guests can hop on and off the wagons at designated stops to explore sixty-five historic buildings, which were found around the state, dismantled, and rebuilt on the complex's 576 acres.

The look is so realistic in each ethnic "community" that even the animal breeds are historically correct to the right century. And the vegetable and herb gardens! Luscious Dunlop strawberries, Latham red raspberries, grapes, pungent dill, crunchy kohlrabi, sweet cucumbers, and other fruits and vegetables are planted in the neatly tended plots. Hops, used for making beer and yeast, grow near several of the German farmhouses. Towering seven-foot-high stands of pole beans sprout in yummy splendor near rows of carrots and radishes.

Just as great-grandpa used to do, the staff of Old World Wisconsin plants and harvests hay, wheat, corn, and rye by hand. On occasion, rattling steam-powered threshers demonstrate how technology speeded up the process. Several acres of harvested rye were used for thatch on the Grube barn and the Koepsell stable, buildings that date to the mid 1850s.

Old World represents almost twenty different ethnic groups, including German, Welsh, Irish, African American, and Bohemian. A crossroads village of the 1870s demonstrates a small community's important social and business elements of the era. The three-story Four-Mile House, a former stagecoach inn, is now a "rooming house." There are also blacksmith and wagon maker's shops where workers go about their daily chores as if they were residents of the town. They prepare meals, paint fences, take care of livestock, and tend crops, generally acting as the original homesteaders would have. Chat with the knowledgeable guides who dress in the appropriate period and ethnic costumes—each of them speaks as a character who might have lived on one of the farms or worked in one of the shops.

The Finnish area of Old World Wisconsin showcases the Rankinen House, which was originally built in 1892 in the Bayfield County town of Oulu and has now been restored to its 1897 style, after a kitchen wing had

A DRIVER EXPERIENCES A ROUGH ROAD IN WESTERN WISCONSIN IN THIS PHOTOGRAPH FROM 1939. (MINNESOTA HISTORICAL SOCIETY)

been added. In addition, several layers of extra logs were also added to the house, providing more headroom to accommodate the early occupants' growing family. The Kortesmaa outhouse nearby is the only such structure preserved at Old World Wisconsin. Other buildings in the Finnish area include a granary, barns, and a sauna.

The Pederson House can be found in the Danish area. It was originally constructed in 1872 in the Polk County town of Luck and has been restored to its 1890s look. When visiting this house, you should note the beams' interesting inverted "V-corner" notching. The queen of Denmark dedicated the Pederson House when she visited Old World in 1976. The Jensen barn in the area dates from 1890. Its dismantled pieces were carried from the town of Laketown in Polk County to be reassembled at Old World.

In the Norwegian area, the Raspberry School, dating from 1896, remains a popular attraction where today's kids can sit on benches and "study" like their forebearers. The building was used until 1914 by Norwegian and Swedish families who lived along frigid Lake Superior's rough-watered Raspberry Bay. The Sorbergshagen barn is one of the more architecturally interesting structures in Old World, with towering corncribs along two of its sides and a drive-through for farm wagons.

The Germanic area's Koepsell House, built in 1858 with a typical half-timbered look, is on the National Register of Historic Places. The nearby Schulz House was constructed in 1856 and is another traditional half-timbered structure. Mud and straw serve as caulking between the beams and side timbers making up the walls.

Even in the winter, Old World Wisconsin offers an adventure. The site has about eight miles of ski trails that meander these glaciated grounds. One short beginner's run is great for kids, beginning at the Ramsey barn. The trail wanders past St. Peter's Church, the first Catholic church built in Milwaukee, and around the Harmony Town Hall. An intermediate loop of about three miles takes skiers literally through the open doors of the Grube threshing barn. Usually, the Raspberry School is open for hot drinks and the occasional cookie. In a concession to modern life, camouflaged toilets are placed along the route. Benches are also provided here and there for tired strollers or skiers.

Your backroads expedition through history at Old World will sweep you into a range of wonderful Wisconsin experiences. You'll learn about geography, the environment, ethnic lifestyles, and the courage, vision, and creativity that it took settle the Badger State. That's part of the fun of poking around along the less-beaten pathways. You might discover something about your own heart and soul, as well.

SUGGESTIONS FOR FURTHER READING

Apps, Jerry. *Cheese: The Making of a Wisconsin Tradition.* Amherst, WI: Amhert Press, 1998.

Bashfield, Jean F. and Conrad R. Stein. *Wisconsin.* Danbury, CT: Children's Press, 1998.

Bell, Chet and Jeanette. *County Parks of Wisconsin: 600 Parks You Can Visit Featuring 25 Favorites.* Black Earth, WI: Trails Books, 1996.

Blei, Norbert, Jean Feraca, Ben Logan, Bob Rashid, Bill Stokes, and George Vukelich. *Wisconsin's Rustic Roads.* Boulder Junction, WI: Lost River Press, 1995.

Davenport, Dave. *Natural Wonders of Wisconsin.* Castine, ME: Country Roads Press, 1995.

Dean, Jill, Howard Mead, and Susan Smith. *Portrait of the Past.* Madison, WI: Wisconsin Tales and Trails, 1998.

Fradin, Dennis Brindell. *Wisconsin.* Chicago, IL: Children's Press, 1992.

Gast, Michele and Byron Glick. *Bed, Breakfast and Bike Western Great Lakes.* Liberty Corner, NJ: Anacus Press, Inc., 2000.

Hailman, Elizabeth D. and Jack Parker. *Backpacking Wisconsin.* Madison, WI: University of Wisconsin Press, 2000.

Hintz, Martin. *Hiking Wisconsin.* Champaign, IL: Human Kinetics, 1997.

Hintz, Daniel and Martin. *Off the Beaten Path: Wisconsin,* 5th edition. Guilford, CT: The Globe Pequot Press, 2002.

Hintz, Martin and Stephen. *Fun With the Family in Wisconsin,* 4th edition. Guilford, CT: The Globe Pequot Press, 2002.

Huhti, Thomas. *Wisconsin.* Emeryville, CA: Avalon Travel Publishing, 2001.

Knowles, Gary G. *The Great Wisconsin Touring Book.* Black Earth, WI: Trail Books, 2000.

Krumm, Bob and Bob Pahula. *52 Wisconsin Weekends: Great Getaways and Adventures for Every Season.* Chicago, IL: NTC Publishing, 1999.

Lisi, Patrick. *Wisconsin Waterfalls, A Touring Guide.* Madison, WI: Prairie Oak Press, 1998.

McBride, Elizabeth and Mike Svob. *Paddling Northern Wisconsin: 82 Great Trips by Canoe and Kayak.* Black Earth, WI: Trails Books, 1998.

Nature Conservancy. *The Places We Save: A Guide to The Nature Conservancy's Preserves in Wisconsin.* Minocqua, WI: Northword Press, Inc., 1997.

Ostergren, Robert C. and Thomas R. Vale. *Wisconsin Land and Life.* Madison, WI: University of Wisconsin Press, 1997.

Rashid, Bob. *Gone Fishing.* Madison, WI: University of Wisconsin Press, 1999.

Richardson, Shawn E. *Biking Wisconsin's Rail Trails.* Cambridge, MN: Adventure Publications, Inc., 1997.

LOGGERS NEAR PARK FALLS, WISCONSIN, PILED THIS LOAD WITH 20,040 FEET OF TIMBER IN THE WINTER OF 1921. (MINNESOTA HISTORICAL SOCIETY)

INDEX

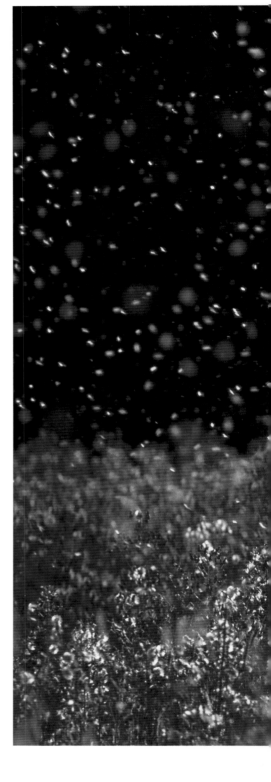

PARACHUTE FRUIT FROM ORANGE HAWKWEED IS SET FREE BY THE WIND ALONG COUNTY ROAD HH, NORTH OF WISCONSIN HIGH-WAY 173.

ABOUT THE AUTHOR AND PHOTOGRAPHER

Award-winning travel journalist Martin Hintz is a true Midwesterner. He grew up in northeast Iowa, and now calls Milwaukee, Wisconsin, home. Hintz has written more than sixty books, which have earned him recognition from the Society of American Travel Writers, the Midwest Travel Writers Association, the Council for Wisconsin Writers, and the prestigious Children's Reading Roundtable. His articles have appeared in many magazines, including *National Geographic World* and *Midwest Living*. In addition to writing about travel, Hintz has also authored books on such eclectic themes as elephant training, motorcycle racing, and Prohibition. He currently serves as the president of the Society of American Travel Writers.

PHOTOGRAPH © BRIAN MALLOY

Bob Rashid has worked as a freelance photographer for more than twenty years. His images have appeared in *Time, Newsweek*, the *New York Times,* and many other publications. A resident of Madison, Wisconsin, Rashid has firsthand experience on the backroads of the Badger State. His career has taken him to more exotic locales as well, including Nicaragua, Scotland, Ukraine, and Kazakhstan. He was among a select group of photographers chosen by the Wisconsin Historical Society to participate in a re-photographic project that resulted in the book, *Wisconsin Then and Now*. Rashid is the photographer of two other books: *Wisconsin's Rustic Roads* and *Gone Fishing*, which he also authored.

PHOTOGRAPH © TINA YAO

1924